REFLECTIONS
OF THE JOURNEY
An Interactive Guide
to Help Individuals
Discover and Sustain Greatness

Manufactured and printed in the United States

ISBN 978-0-9858793-0-3

Cover design, editing, and layout by
WhiteHorse Industries

PARENTAL ADVISORY
RICH CONTENT
APPROPRIATE LANGUAGE
LIFE-LONG SUCCESS

REFLECTIONS
OF THE JOURNEY

An Interactive Guide
to Help Individuals
Discover and Sustain Greatness

…Choose to Succeed!

Kevin Harris, Ed.D.

How To Successfully Use This Book

There is no time like the present. Especially when individuals are thinking about asking the tough questions but, often freeze up at critical times; afraid of the short list of possible answers. It is with deep conviction that I inform you that my work is not separate from how I live my life. I discovered Kevin Harris while on this journey of scholarship. As a result, I have learned to create answers, as opposed to accepting the obvious choices that are presented to the inner city young black male. Although these elements existed in my immediate environment the majority of my life, my vision for living was not distorted by this truth, but enhanced it significantly.

You are about to read and discover the truth about a significant person. That person is you the reader. This book was created to help individuals contribute to their academic achievement, personal development, self-actualization, survival, and success in life. *Reflections of the Journey...* provides moral perspectives and practical strategies for individuals and organizations to improve. It provides an overall blueprint on how individuals can improve internally, develop a positive attitude, seek the appropriate guidance, set personal goals, understand the process of improving, and moreover, to help individuals begin with the end in mind. In addition, it was important for me to acknowledge and thank several people who have contributed to and enriched my life, particularly my academic and football careers. I wanted to publicly thank all of you in this book.

This book is structured interactively, such that each reader must adhere to what is being asked of him or her. You, the reader, must follow the directions and take action toward improvements to experience success. This book provides tools and improvement plans for you to fill in the blanks, based upon personal goals and aspirations in all areas where growth is needed, and it focuses on the areas of academic achievement and personal development.

I listed many elements in this book that were important and relevant to my journey. For example, I love reading and listening to music. It is important to note that after every chapter you will find a suggested reading list and music selection list (radio edited versions). When listening to the music selections, focus only on the instrumentation—the beat—not on the lyrics. Not all readers will read the suggested texts and listen to the suggested music. My philosophy on reading is that "I will out *read* you; therefore, I will out *lead* you." I included some of my favorite poems and quotes as well. The objective here is for you to find what is close and dear to your heart and utilize those elements as essentials while on your personal journey.

There are objectives at the beginning of each chapter to provide direction for the reader. At the conclusion of each chapter the reader will be required to complete the open response assignments. These assignments require critical thought and a careful analysis of what is being asked of the reader.

When you are clear of your path and your direction in life, you must work to make improvements everyday, while being honest with yourself about your outcomes. This book is a self-help guide that requires you to seek others to assist you. However, you, the reader, must be consistent and relentless while working on improvements. See the Harris Choose to Succeed Framework and the Core Student Standards as frameworks to facilitate greatness and personal reform.

This book is required reading for <u>anyone</u> who is interested in individual success or success for their group/organization through self-actualization and personal transformation. By anyone, I mean elementary, middle, high school, and college students; CEOs, COOs and entrepreneurs; and faith- and community-based organizations. This book is affirming and motivational. It provides symbolic images of what is important to me.

Objective

When you adhere to the steps and action plans, you will change and grow while on your journey. This is not a book to read. It is an interactive guide that challenges you to internalize the text and go beyond the established norms of what may be ordinary to that which is extraordinary living.

Questions

Do you believe in yourself and your potential?

Are you producing the results that you want?

Are you satisfied with where you are in life?

What drives you?

What do you want in and out of life?

When you answer these questions, your journey to discover and sustain greatness will begin. You are the architect and ultimately responsible for your academic achievement and personal development, as well as the setbacks and failures. Choose to succeed and become the person you aspire to become. Above all, I hope this book encourages you to seriously examine and analyze one's self and map out an action plan toward a life-changing transformation.

Enjoy the Journey.

Table of Contents

ROLE MODEL
Not President Obama. Not Tiger Woods.
Not Jay-Z. Not even Elmo.
Simply Dad.

CPSIA information can be obtained
at www.ICGtesting.com
Printed in the USA
FFOW01n0549210217
32658FF

9 780985 879303

Foreword

Through the years of the past century, many writers, thinkers, sociologists, and psychologists have rendered their assessments of the pathology of the African-American community, particularly where the male members of the community are concerned. From the seminal work of W.E.B. Dubois in Souls of Black Folks, through Gunnar Myrdal's An American Dilemma, through the exemplary work of Kenneth Clark, and through the esteem-building efforts of Jawanza Kunjufu, great minds and determined wills have appraised the condition of the Black male landscape, and have offered commentary, critique, and macro-solutions to the pathology of the African-American male. Now comes a book that, quite frankly, offers real and practical solutions to the plight of those persons who are mired in the mud of misguided achievement.

Dr. Kevin Harris has brought forward a paradoxical glimpse of life, and what it is going to take to march onward and upward toward the prize. Though autobiographical in tone, it is a story that is about everyone who has faced adversity. Though one has the keen sense that the hand that holds his pen is that of a Black man, his perspective can readily be embraced by anyone seeking to do more and be more tomorrow than yesterday. Though it is clear that Dr. Harris is comfortable in the community of intellectual achievement, his common sense guide embraces rather than chases away the "Brother on the Block." While he makes great use of the language of proven notions of distant sages, he effectively brings front and center the challenges of 21st century life navigation, even employing the discourse of contemporary youth culture. It is hard to know whether the prescience presented is steeped in the tried and true wisdom of Mordecai Johnson, or the wit of Jay-Z.

All of us who have walked the planet for more than just a little while will recognize that his journey is not unlike our journey, and his challenges are challenges all of us have faced. Dr. Harris has, however, done more than just point his finger and curse the darkness. He seeks to light a candle that, when embraced, will light the path for any and all who make the choice to "choose wisely." Success, left to be defined by the aspirations of the reader, personally or in broad application, is indeed incumbent upon the connection of a series of wise choices. The Harris Choose to Succeed Framework even gives you the instrument with which to benchmark your success.

This is a good read. Moreover, it is an excellent guide for fruitful, bountiful, and principled living. Enjoy your journey.

Roi T. Johnson
Principal Partner, Gordian Group Solutions, Inc.

Dedication

To my son Kevin, Jr.: Holding and guiding you is the biggest blessing I could ever receive and more precious than anything I ever imagined! You are my reflection eternal. My work in the global community is with deep conviction and it comes full circle back to you.

As you travel to find, define, and redefine your purpose in life, stand in solidarity with fraternal order as a means of protection and guidance. Practice restraint when faced with opportunities that will lead to short-term happiness, but long-term misery. Research your future projections and become knowledgeable and well-read in the industry. Walk with your head high and work at a pace that is 50% faster and 100% more efficient than everybody else. Your enthusiasm will draw positive and negative people to you—follow the positive people. Exhibit discernment and nerve to move forward with what you must do to raise your level of discourse and world view.

Understand that it is your duty to live your life in the light of good and love. Your scholarship apex will determine to what extent you can help yourself, but more importantly, to what extent your family and other worthy people can be helped. Utilize the ingenuity that you possess to distinguish and reveal yourself to a greater societal cause. Perseverance is the only option when you are faced with quandary. Our friendship is more sacred than you can imagine, so live right by good will and with purpose. Continue your quest for high aspirations, even if it means that you have to travel to the darkest places and the highest peaks and lowest valleys while on this planet. Look within yourself for truth, strength, and salvation. Accepting the truth will set you free mentally, spiritually, intellectually, and financially. Immediately establish new endeavors after achieving your short-term and long-term goals.

Never lower your level of respect for your mother, anybody else's mother, yourself, and all other people whom you fully embrace. Live your life nobly and give more of yourself by practicing purpose everyday! Your meta-cognition will give you clarity and purity to your everyday thoughts. Exercise every physical, mental, and intellectual muscle and fabric in your mind, body, and soul, because it is you who represents the youth. You are a strong one—strong in will power and in political leadership. Build nations my son; your return on investment is your returning to where you are from to empower people to succeed!

I love you, Kevin Harris, Jr.
Your Big Dad!
June 3, 2011

*Our lives begin to end
the day we become silent about things that matter.*
– Dr. Martin Luther King, Jr.

Acknowledgements

I am thankful for the many blessings thus far in my life. It is and always will be my plan that I must continue to execute the highest level of service to others while I am here on this planet. To my grandparents, Thommie Sr. and Minnie Harris, your teachings and discipline are so much appreciated. Our discussions continue to serve me every day as I make meaning of my continuous development. I am most thankful for you teaching me how to be caring, unselfish, open to new ideas, and how to use discernment.

I thank my father and mother Clyde Frazier and Liz Harris. To my five sisters (Nancy, Michelle, Sheila, Darla, & Claudia) thank you for the foundational support. Growing up the only brother taught me a lot about how women feel and deal with tragedy and triumph. To my nieces and nephews Chelle, Andre', Nae, DeAndre', Nae, Chanel, Keith, Daria, Khalli, Anthony, and Kaden, I believe in all of you and love you more than you can ever imagine! To the Harris family, thank you for all the support and understanding of my unconquerable soul. I am grateful and blessed to be part of a fine family that was built on general principles of Thommie Harris, Sr., respect, loyalty, and discipline.

Special thanks to *Pops Boys-The Harris Boys* (Velt, Bey, Herb, Art, Mick, Donnie, and Curt) Chuck, Tom-TH III, Little Donnie, Big Q, and Big Mike.

Special thank you to Ricardo Teamor, to Eleanor Hopkins, to the Wilson, Lane, Williams, Winford, Robinson, Tate, Diggs, Workman, Rice, Blakely, Frazier, Claytor, Nadel, and Young families; Aunt Nell, Aunt Vera, Aunt Darlene, Annissa and Elise Harris, April Hart, Henry Marzette, Garcia Lane, Leon Williams, Lisa Harris, Lil Frank, Net Lane, Uncle Andy Lane, Flo Harris, Pat & Bruce Winford, El Jay, Cheryl Wilson, Wendy Wilson, Robin & Eric, Ju Ju, Irma Davis, Leroy Williams, Roy Donaldson, Hutch Campbell, Ivan Williams, Richard Williams, Ced & HJ, Claude Bentley, Cork & Ronnie Wilson, Dave Wilson, (the late R. "Lamar" Wilson, Kevin Workman, Kevin Anderson & James Clinkscale), John Blakely, Ralph Workman, (Kev, Delbert, and Tony Jack), Lenny Wilson, Kevin Sledge, Mike Wright, Arsenia Richardson, Van Staples, Darnell Green, Keith Griffin, Big O, Derrick & Richard Thomas, Ronnie Howard, Lamar Boone, Brian Jones, Rob Owens, Devlin Culiver, Alvin Jenkins, Craig Walker, Daniel Escobar, Damon & Keith Winford, Mark & Kenny Overton, Sam & Dwayne Stanford, Tony & Kenny Donaldson, Brian Kopp, Brian Marrow, Willie Green, Tony Robinson, Dave Slaina, Tom Rogers, Brian Mauzy, Salt, Hayes, McCurdy, Sterling & Tony Haywood, Dennis & Terrance Mosley, Steve Lyle, Earl Sykes, Terry Pierson, T. Lee Chism, Wendell Stewart, Marcus Gordon, Rob Echols, Derrick & Keith Brown, Carlos Hall, Billy Williams, Thomas Spann, Curtis Morgan, Maurice Bass, T. Tubbs, Pam Hubbard, Chuck Fitzgerald, John Gore, Al Craig, Sean Patton, Ramon Amil, Sammy G., Steven Scales, Dexter Davis, Randy Hicks, Seti Richardson, Revs. Lonnie & Kenny Simon, Pastor Mack Hannah, Jessica Horne, and Artie Kramer, Chuck Sammarone, Mack Gilchrist, Dwayne Watson, Robert Leflore.

Many thanks to Dr. RC Saravanabhavan, Dr. Lois Harrison-Jones, Dr. Russell Jackson, the late Dr. Jerome B. Jones, Dr. Dawn Williams, Dr. Dia Sekayi, Dr. Peter Sola, Dr. Vinetta Jones, Dr. Wade Boykin, Dr. Mary Hoover, Dr. Will Johnson, former president H. Patrick Swygert, Dean Bill Keene, G-SAC Peers and (Cohort I – Dr. Grillo, Dr. Cadet, Dr. Woodson, and Dr. Hampton), Dr. Alvin Thornton, Dr. Donna McDaniel, Quentin R. Lawson, Dr. Charlie Mae Knight, Fred Dean, Dr. Carol & Franklin Shelton, Wilson Bland, Dr. Sandra Dupree, Dr. Jamie Wyche, Dr. Eric Mays, Dr. Franklin Chambers III, Joe Emmanuel, Carolyn Smith, Office of Residence Life/Cook Hall Staff and the entire Howard University faculty and staff (2002-2005).

Westlake Families: Thomas, Boone, Jr. Allen, Mr. Pepsi, Anderson, Overton, Frazier, Howard,

Jones, Borkins, Bankston, McLendon, Clinkscale, Rudolph, Green, Spann, Dumas, Walker, Jenkins, Rutledge, Morgan, Graham, (Lynn, Brian, and Johnny Murray) Stanford, and McGloughton families. Mike Ivey, Kevin Talley, Jamon Gilbert, John Randall, Blaine Griffin, Joe Teague, Antonio Miller, Ira Cross, George White, Marcus Edwards, Deollo Anderson, Buster Stanley, Dre Finley, 226 Family: Jake, Mark, Ed, Frankie, Jamie, Curt, Matt, Fonz, Tat, Sue, Lauren, Cindy, Mike & Jauan Young, B. Teague, D. Wiley, Johnnie Foster, Byrd, Chipper, Mark Staples, the late Keith Stanford, Jerome Johnson, & Steve Novak, Darnell Tate, Spive, Queener, Rob MC, Aaron Sanders, K. Matlock, Jerry & Brad, Jeef, Big Ken, J. Markovich, Vince Ricotelli, Massiomi, Tom Orr and the A TEAM: Keels, McFerrin, Watts and Bass.

Brothers Reggie Carson, John Howard, William Blackwell, Jesse Peeples, Drs. Travis & Travan Jasper, Harry Manning, Larry Rasberry, Dr. Marc Harrigan, Michael Moore, Nakia Shaw, Roi Johnson, Patrick Tolbert, Manus Caldwell, Jr., Samuel Bell, Jr., Quan Smith, Dr. LaVelle Miller, Bruce Demps, Dr. Bruce Hines, Dr. Cleve Taylor, Wendell Spann, Bryson Thompson, Donald Martin, Tim Brown, Jerome Dawson, Vontell Johnson, Lydell Clark, John Ray, Dr. Patrick Antoine, Reginald High, Patrick Daniel, Kenny Howard, Sean Mack, Dr. Elton Holden, Shareem Brown, Walter Dula, Darwin Newton, Charles Dubissette, Dr. Travis Paige, Ryan Stewart, Darrell Dial, Michael Sims, Chuck Wicks, Dave Alford, Gerard Sanders, Dave Cook, Micah Hines, Javin Rudolph, Steve Haynes, Keith Thompson, Alfred Forbes IV, Mike Dula, Greg Fields, Skip Watson, Wesley Murphy, Kevin Roulac, Jron Collier, Larry Johnson, Sean Griffin, Jason Frazier, Poppa Joe, Rashad Hodges, Kenneth Joe, Dom Bouchelion, Ernest Harvey, Jimmy Thomas, Carl Bacon, James Byrd, Wendell Robinson, Broderick Smiley, Dunlap, Greg Evans, Derrick Austin, Dr. Carl McNair, Craig Fitz, Kevin Payton, Dr. Terrance Menefee, Craig Harper, Omar Williams, Bam, Allen Settles, D. Jolly, Demo, Thee, D. Love, Terry, Hakeem, Dr. Ray Hill, Dewberry, Corey Jarvis, Gerald Barber, Harry Johnson, Mike Merrell, Ron Baptiste, Warren Cray, T. Madison, Jamie Younger, Dr. George McElroy, Dr. Rob Robbins, Casey Landsman, Dr. Marvin Pryor, Nelson Render, Jerry Fordham, Bill Thomas & the entire brotherhood of Omega Psi Phi Fraternity, Inc. 1911.

Special thanks to Cathy O'Donnell, Coaches Dick Crum, Jon Hoke, Ricky Porter, Bob Stoops, Kenny Long, Ligs, Decker, Fish, Mahoney, Perry Fewell, Tressel, Dantonio, and Cordelli; Linda Zigmund, John Faulstick, Dean Rouser, Dr. Fran Dorsey, Dr. Edward Crosby, Dr. E. Timothy Moore, the late Dr. Wiley Smith, Dr. Barnes-Harden, Prof. Johnnie Miller, the late Dr. Adamle, former President Dr. Carol Cartwright, Keith Younger, Sean Patterson, Vance Benton, Troy Robinson, Michael Hedrick, Brian Dusho, Waverly Willis, B.A., Dr. Brian Amison, Patrick Young, Larry Long, Rodney West, Paul Haynes, Roger Jones, Jeff Turner, Broderick, Matt Jenne, Ryan Creed, Renners, Steve Taggs, Guy Decker, (the late Victor Smith, Donnie Cantrell, & Matt Ramser), EJ, Berk Jr., Morrey Norris, Joe Brown, Brad Smith, Ripasky, Kinnebrew, Kenny Parker, John Jack, Clem, Mark Porter, Shuman, PJ Allen, Woody, Danny Ford, Andy Harmon, Agnew, Tkatch, Stenning, Dr. Roger Terry, LD Hartman, Brian Overbey, Tony & Mark Britt, DJ, Nick Petty, Cook, Ted Gregory, Mo Sumpter, Marcus Haywood, John Taylor, Acie, Phil Thompson, Marion Styles, Eric Beasley, and all the coaches, staff, teammates, and the Oscar Ritchie staff at Kent State University (1989-1994).

Thank you to all the people from (Sunday School Teachers at New Bethel Baptist Church, Little Braves, Little Redmen, & Covington Elementary school teachers). Coaches: John Kopp, Lodyn, Banks, Kish, Robinson, Repko, Senedak, Wainewright, Koma, and Clarrett. Principal-Mrs. Marinelli, Mr. Jeff Covington, Mr. G. Mrs. Benford, Mr. Anania, Mrs. Chambers, Mrs. Donlin, Falgiani, Caparso, Mrs. Kunze, Mr. Elias, Mrs. McDonough, Mrs. Ponzo, Mrs. Thompson, Mr. Zarlenga, and the entire student body, faculty, and staff from Youngstown Woodrow Wilson High School (1985-1989).

Prologue

Four Little Secrets

1. Go to uncharted territory to find and redefine yourself. Adversity reintroduces you to yourself.
2. Your attitude, ideals, and expectations are three silent elements that speak loudest about you.
3. Discipline yourself now, so that no one has to punish you later.
4. Anchor yourself in your integrity and family.

If
by Rudyard Kipling

If you can keep your head when all about you are losing theirs and blaming it on you; If you can trust yourself when all men doubt you, But make allowance for their doubting too: If you can wait and not be tired by waiting, Or, being lied about, don't deal in lies, Or being hated don't give way to hating, And yet don't look too good, nor talk too wise;

If you can dream---and not make dreams your master; If you can think--- and not make thoughts your aim, If you can meet with Triumph and Disaster And treat those two impostors just the same:. If you can bear to hear the truth you've spoken Twisted by knaves to make a trap for fools, Or watch the things you gave your life to, broken,And stoop and build'em up with worn-out tools;

If you can make one heap of all your winnings And risk it on one turn of pitch-and-toss, And lose, and start again at your beginnings, And never breathe a word about your loss:

If you can force your heart and nerve and sinew To serve your turn long after they are gone, And so hold on when there is nothing in you Except the Will which says to them: "Hold on!"

If you can talk with crowds and keep your virtue, Or walk with Kings---nor lose the common touch, If neither foes nor loving friends can hurt you, If all men count with you, but none too much:

If you can fill the unforgiving minute With sixty seconds' worth of distance run, Yours is the Earth and everything that's in it, And---which is more---you'll be a Man, my son!

The ultimate measure of a man is not where he stands
in moments of comfort and convenience, but where he stands
at times of challenge and controversy.
– Dr. Martin Luther King, Jr. *Strength to Love* (1963)

You are at a crossroad; now make a decision!

Introduction

We can, wherever and whenever we choose, successfully teach all children whose schooling is of interest to us. We already know more than we need to do that. Whether or not we do it must finally depend on how we feel about the fact that we haven't so for.
–Ron Edmonds (1979)

Today our schools are more segregated than when the historic 1954 Brown vs. Board of Education landmark United States Supreme court decision declared state laws establishing separate public schools for black and white students unconstitutional. The decision stated, "Separate educational facilities are inherently unequal." The decision overturned the Plessy vs. Ferguson decision of 1896 which allowed state sponsored segregation. In turn, dejure racial segregation was ruled a violation of the Equal Protection Clause of the Fourteenth Amendment of the United States Constitution. As a result, integration and the civil rights movement were established.

Today we are in a far worse predicament than when the Nation at Risk report was released in April 1983. Some of the critical issues examined at that time are the same issues that continue to negatively impact our educational system today (ill-prepared students and low achievement scores nationally and internationally). Moreover, African Americans exhibit double-digit deficiencies in just about every measurable category (i.e., test scores, graduation rates, and reading and math proficiency). Ironically, as a nation with unmatched K-12 and collegiate educational resources, we trail other nations by double digits in both math and science and, our literacy rates are abysmal.

Today we are continuously experimenting with education reform models that purport to be the answer to many of the urban pathologies that exist in our public schools (gaps between and among race, class, gender, and economics relative to suspensions, expulsions, failure rates, education attainment, special education vs. gifted programs, and tracking). However, low expectations for achievement and low standards of accountability have contributed to pity and empathy for students, which often produce excuses and negative outcomes from the students, staff, and the school/school system leaders.

...its hard but its fair.
– John Howard, 6-03-Mighty YΣ

Furthermore, many African American students that I have had the privilege to teach and lead as a former teacher and high school principal perceive the nation's public schools as "fall through spots" that perpetuate the socialization and tracking to nowhere. At some point during this process, we have gradually accepted lower standards and little-to-no expectations. It is my assertion that change in public education will not happen until we raise the standards and expectations of the students that we serve. Our students are in need of a paradigm shift that is tangible, touchable, observable, and sustainable.

According to Sowell (1974), *"Schools are remembered as having atmospheres where support, encouragement, and rigid standards combine to enhance students' self-worth and increase their aspirations to achieve. In addition, he highlighted the fact that prominent educator, Dr. Faustine Jones, provides a portrait of the historical Dunbar High School –affectionately known as the Notable M Street High School Alum: the Honorable Dr. Oscar J. Cooper (1888-1972) and the Honorable Professor Frank Coleman (1890-1967), M Street High School (Washington, DC). According to her survey results, teachers didn't give students a choice between learning and not learning—failure to learn was unacceptable to teachers, family, peers, and the community. The choice was how much one would learn and what subjects would be mastered."*

It is evident that we are facing a major crisis in the world's economy. The impact of the (1) high dropout rate in high school, (2) the small percentage of students who hold a bachelor's degree, (3) the increasing percentage of students who require remedial courses at the collegiate level, and (4) the ever increasing matriculation into the prison systems for African Americans is a frightening reality for our economy and society in general. These four areas represent a negative cost center that absorbs waning resources with little to no return on investment. Globally, the United States ranks far behind other industrial nations in college students studying and mastering science, technology, engineering, and math. As it relates to African Americans, we are already competing from a deficit. It is not that we cannot compete, the question raised here is, what are we competing for? When you lower student and parent expectations, you are almost guaranteed to finish in last place. When you are training for last place, how can you not finish in last place? Success for African American students is predicated on predictable outcomes that are rooted in high expectations, resources, training, accountability, support, and self-actualization. Without these elements, we can predict negative outcomes.

Man's main task in life is to give birth to himself.
– Eric Fromm

The Blue Note

I wrote this book as a back drop to how I continuously tap into my inner self by listening and responding to the *blue note*. I define the blue note as my ways, means, and actions that I take as a result of the beats and melodies that exist, but which many fail to hear or to listen for. I am not a rapper, singer, musician, or a composer of music. However, I continue to pay homage to many instrumental pieces through which I create my own mental songs to help me get through my challenges, accomplish my goals, and add to my perspective on life. Music was always important as I was growing up. During my early childhood, I recall listening to Andre Crouch, The Mississippi Mass Choir, and Earth, Wind, and Fire. As I listened to the music, I often found myself looking at the many Earth, Wind, and Fire album covers trying to figure out what all the symbols meant. These listening activities stimulated my thoughts, as I attempted to make sense of my own inferences, observations, interpretations, and correlations between their music and the Egyptian, hieroglyphic, and Greek symbols on their album covers. Most of the good music of today is kept away from our youth primarily because of the parental advisory stickers attached to the records. With these stickers affixed to these records, the listeners await with high anticipation the negative words or messages within the records and miss the extraordinary music. I do not recall any album covers in my mother's or grandparents' household that had parental advisory labels affixed to them. As an adult, I buy certain music simply for the *blue note*. There are countless opinions about most of the lyrics that are considered part of mainstream music. However, this music often times is genius! I am influenced by the *blue note* which captures my imagination and allows me to get beyond some of the opinions and pseudo lyrics. I enjoy music with social messages. Furthermore, I appreciate understanding the meaning of my experiences through listening to jazz, symphony, and hip-hop instrumentals.

Students today need to know that the expectations for them have been raised by the adults who have raised expectations for themselves. Today I take a bold and daring position in recommending and effecting change. This change will provide our students with a philosophical and psychological directive to move them to internally grasp the creative renewable energy and reveal the star that each of them aspires to become. However, due to the lack of consistency and continuity, the internal flame grows weaker over time. Student Reform and core student standards are essential. These two important elements will support the paradigm shift from students who are contributing to broken systems, to students who are choosing to succeed!

It has been well documented that society, in general, continuously gives credence to the negative aspects of individual student profiles, i.e., test scores, socio-economic status, class, and race. It appears that we have established an association of romanticism with urban pathologies and urban school youth. Today I reflect on our failures from the past—ready to actively engage students in the development process of Student Reform and core student standards.

You have an opportunity to right your own ship, but it will require accountability and a true passion exhibited by high expectations which you MUST embody for yourself. This will also directly influence how you think about yourself and your future.

This publication serves as a moral and ethical imperative for you to invest in your own personal development as a prerequisite to academic achievement and life-long success. May the power be vested in ten two-letter words: if it is to be, it is up to me. It is up to you to choose to succeed!

You can't buy success, but you will pay significantly
for not choosing to succeed.
– author unknown

What Are You Worth?

This is not a question of socio-economic status or family income. Your answer to this vitally important question will reflect the level of your self-actualization. If you have a positive perception of your self-worth, then you are considered to have high self-esteem. If so, your response will likely be characterized by self-confidence, optimism, assertiveness, eagerness, affection, independence, truth, enthusiasm, ingenuity, ability to handle criticism, emotional maturity, nerve, intelligence, and an accurate assessment of your skills, abilities, and talents.

On the other end of the spectrum, if you have a negative judgment of your self-worth, then your low self-esteem is likely to be characterized by self-doubt, passive aggressiveness, isolation, sensitivity to criticism, short temperedness, procrastination, distrust, and a lack of courage, aspiration, and truth. You may also engage in behaviors, such as using illegal substances and drinking alcohol, that will impair your mind and body. For starters, to be considered a worthy person is synonymous with having morals, ethics, vision, and a plan.

You must first establish a network of people that contributes to your net worth. Surround yourself with people who are dedicated to uplifting individuals who have a desire to become great thinkers, doctors, lawyers, educators, and philanthropists. Surround yourself with mentors and peers who provide support yet demand realistic expectations. You may lose some things along your journey, but you should never lose your integrity! Having integrity will help you eliminate a network of people who do not contribute to your net worth. The most credible, reliable, and accurate instrument available to measure your self-worth is the mirror. The mirror will only reflect what you put in front of it. Look in the mirror and reflect daily.

Ecological Self-Assessment: The Start of My Ending

An ecological self-assessment consists of monitoring the current and changing conditions of the internal and external environment from which one's past, current, and future successes or failures can be assessed and evaluated. You must fully understand the structure and function of your environment to develop, improve, and succeed. It is critical that you develop a foundation that is environmentally friendly, in which multiple paths can be carved from your choices and experiences. You must avoid personally-induced stress. You must understand that things that come easy often have unexpected consequences. Any goal worth achieving requires hard work. Develop survival strategies and success strategies to help you drive your decisions as you travel in mind and in time. Your objective is three-fold: (1) acknowledge who you are; (2) build upon your strengths and potential; and (3) make great use of the resources around you.

My Personal and Suggested Readings and Instrumental Music Selections

READ

Carson, B. (1990). *Gifted Hands*. New York: Harper Collins.

Dixson, Adrienne & Rousseau Celia K. (2006). *Critical Race Theory in Education*. New York: Rutledge.

Hurston, L. (2004). *Speak, So You Can Speak Again: The Life of Zora Neal Hurston*. New York: Doubleday.

Winbush, D. L. (1995). *The Complete Kwaanza: Celebrating our Cultural Harvest*. New York: HarperCollins.

LISTEN

Alicia Keys; *Troubles*

Earth, Wind, & Fire; *Be Ever Wonderful*

CHAPTER
1

THE MAKING OF YOU:
KOS (KNOWLEDGE OF SELF)
AND UNDERSTANDING

I'm not where I want to be, but I'm not where I used to be.
– Dr. Rapheal G. Warnock, Ph.D., Pastor
Historic Ebenezer Baptist Church, Atlanta, GA

Objectives

At the completion of this chapter
you will be able to:

List ways to improve your self-image

Identify four factors that contribute to your
uniqueness and growth cycle

Perspective

You are a special person. No other person on this planet is like you. You have unique swagger and a unique look. You act differently, think differently, and politic differently from others. You are extraordinary! Acknowledge your uniqueness, but more importantly, know that all other people are special too and have been created to serve a specific purpose on this planet as well. It is essential that you learn and understand four key elements that contribute to your uniqueness. These elements include your belief system, cultural heritage, environment, and self-image.

Belief System

Your belief system is what shapes your morals and values. I strongly recommend that you read and research all the elements that shape your belief system. I also recommend that you obtain as much accurate information on as many generational family members as possible and create a family tree. This exercise will allow you to keep up with the traditions, values, and belief system of the family as an institution. People have been known to develop their belief system based upon their cultural, political, and other affiliations. Understand that your belief system will guide your thinking and dictate your actions. Believe in yourself and that you can accomplish your goals. Believe that you are somebody special. Believe that your purpose is meaningful and that you strive for improvement everyday. Believe in your choice to succeed!

Cultural Heritage

Without a doubt, your ideals are strongly influenced by your cultural heritage. It is important for you to understand how your cultural heritage makes you special. It is important for you to have a deep understanding of yourself and then to learn about other cultures. Learned behaviors, beliefs, and norms are passed down through generations. It is important to note that appropriate and inappropriate behaviors are learned behaviors. Foods, dances, holidays, and family traditions represent your culture. You, like all other people develop good traits and characteristics; likewise you develop bad ones. People exhibit good characteristics and bad characteristics. You are more likely to represent the characteristic or trait that you feed the most! Do NOT obey a thirst for unhealthy living choices.

Environment

People generally demonstrate and stand in solidarity when it comes to their neighborhood. People take pride when they yell with enthusiasm: I'm from Brooklyn, the ATL, or Y-Town. Things have become more personal, because shout-outs have now been further localized to more specific communities such as: E. 117 & St. Clair, SWATS, or The Hill 10304—it's endless. In every American city, an identity has been created that has a greater influence on how inner city kids identify with their environment. The environment has a DNA of its own, and the individuals in these environments are representatives of a subculture that contributes to society at-large. Two elements, the physical and the psychological, have a strong influence on your personal development.

Your physical environment is made up of all the elements around you. The main element is the place where you live. Regardless of where you reside, you have no control of your physical environment, but you do control your actions which contribute positively or negatively to your environment.

Your psychological environment is made up of the mental intangibles exhibited by those around you. It includes the internal DNA and the feelings and beliefs of your family members, school personnel, students and friends at your school and in your neighborhood. One thing to note is that your choice of friends is influenced by your psychological perspective on how you see yourself and all the elements around you. Choose your friends, carefully!

Tell me who your friends are, and I'll tell you who YOU are.
– Marian C. Jackson, mother of eight and woman of wisdom

Self-Image

Regardless of how much you can remember, your self-image started at an early age. Your self-image is largely influenced by the people around you and how you internalize their behaviors and actions. Your self-image is forever evolving. You can improve your self-image by learning to deal with negative issues and by making desired changes.

There are two things you need to do to start improving your self-image.

1. **Be realistic about your expectations of yourself**
   Remember that you are unique, but you are not perfect. Establish a balance in your life, because you will do some things as well as others and other things not as well as other people. Remember, you are not better than anyone, but you must give your best in all that you do.

2. **Continuously work on developing and enhancing your talents and abilities**
   Developing and enhancing your talents and abilities will help you improve your self-image. Use the talents and abilities that you were given to contribute to something greater than yourself. Remember, talent means nothing without continuous practice.

NO EXCUSES!

Excuses are tools of the incompetent. They build monuments of nothing.
Those who specialize in them seldom accomplish anything.

Growing up in Westlake, the inner city of Youngstown, Ohio was good and bad. The bad part was that this place had all of the elements and pathologies that many poor inner cities across America have today: poverty, high unemployment, crime, drugs, and violence. The good part was that you learned about respect and it was one of the consistent elements in life that kids were taught when I was growing up. I recall the time when I was in fifth grade and my mother moved us from the north side to the south side of town. I had to find my way around the new neighborhood. It was different, because I missed the established norms from my previous neighborhood. I remember joining a different little league football team and serving as the football manager for the high school, Woodrow Wilson High School. Our high school football team possessed some pretty good talent, but there was great talent all over the city. We were not posting winning seasons during that time. In the off-season, when I was entering my freshmen year of high school, I reported to weight lifting practice with fire and determination in my eyes. I told Head Coach John Kopp that I was going to be the greatest player that he ever coached and that our team would post winning seasons prior to my graduation.

I did everything I could to get the best talent in our school to play football. Many guys who possessed great talent chose not to play. In spite of this, we built a good team around our core players and put victories together. Many guys went on to play college football and to graduate from college as well. Out of that group, a few guys even completed post-graduate studies earning masters, law, medical, and doctoral degrees.

During that time in my life one could not hide behind excuses. It was important to get out in front of life with a plan or to have an exit strategy from the "hood" to enter and graduate from college. I cannot thank my supporting cast enough for being tough on me. From that tough love I developed a spirit of continuous drive. I had a lot of adult family members and close friends who could provide multiple answers and examples for the "would haves, could haves, and should haves." There was just simply no excuse. Success was, and still is, the only option.

Kevin Harris is a throwback to the old-style single-wing triple threat. He led the city league in total offense with 1,795 yards including 849 passing and 846 rushing. He led the city league in scoring with 90 points including 10 touchdowns, 15 PAT's and 5 field goals. He was third in the league in punting with a 33.5 average. He also kicked off. On defense, he registered 38 tackles, 32 assists and intercepted 3 passes while playing limited defense. In his junior year, he passed for more than 1,300 yards and rushed for more than 400 yards. Harris is third in school history in interceptions posting 12 interceptions in his 4 year high school career while only playing defense 30 percent of the time. An outstanding leader who bench presses 315 pounds and squats 650. He has 4.5 speed and a vertical leap of 34 inches. He was the best pure athlete on a football field in my 23 years of coaching.
–Head Football Coach John Kopp
Youngstown Woodrow Wilson High School (1988)

I give a lot of credit and credence to my gridiron experiences that taught me some basic success and survival strategies for life. I give even more credit to my grandparents for taking my sisters and me to service every Sunday in the very early stages of my life.

I was born on defense, so I had to create some offense; early exposure to wisdom encouraged me to practice my importance.
– Rick Ross, (2009)

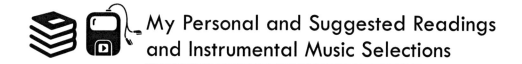 My Personal and Suggested Readings and Instrumental Music Selections

READ

Akbar, Na'im. (1998). *Know Thy Self.* Tallahassee: Mind Productions & Associates.

Akbar, Na'im. (1985). *The Community of Self (Revised).* Tallahassee: Mind Productions &Associates.

Karenga, M. (1997). *Kwanzaa: A Celebration of Family, Community and Culture (Commemorative).* Los Angeles: University of Sankore Press.

Kunjufu, Jawanza. (1984). *Developing Positive Self Images & Discipline in Black Children.* Chicago: African American Images.

Hartness, J. & Eskelin, N. (1993). *The 24-Hour-Turnaround: Discovering the Power to Change.* Grand Rapids: Baker Book House Company.

LISTEN

Adele; *My Hometown Glory*

Anthony Hamilton; *Comin' Where I'm From*

Curtis Mayfield; *The Making of You*

Groove Theory; *Come Home*

Outkast; *You May Die*

Wynton Marsalis and Art Blakley; *Webb City*

9th Wonder; *Heaven Sent*

9th Wonder; *This Normal Sin*

9th Wonder; *Visionary*

Chapter 1 represents the beginning of the rest of your life.

The following questions represent LIFEWORK! While in school, you are assigned homework, but these are the questions that you must ask and answer for yourself every day of your life. Identify strategies and techniques you can adopt and utilize to improve your self-image.

1. What is your perception of yourself?

2. Name at least four elements that contribute to your uniqueness.

3. Who are the individuals who can/will help you build your personal growth cycle?

4. Ask yourself, "Who am I?" The real answer will be revealed, when you face adversity.

Chapter 1 Action Item
How would you describe yourself?

Provide a detailed summary explanation of yourself within the context of your self-image and your uniqueness. This summary should represent a personal profile in narrative form.

_____

_____

_____

_____

_____

_____

_____

_____

_____

_____

_____

_____

_____

_____

_____

_____

_____

_____

_____

_____

_____

_____

_____

_____

_____

_____

_____

_____

_____

_____

_____

_____

_____

_____

_____

_____

_____

_____

CHAPTER
2

CONSTRUCTING INFLUENCES ON YOUR PERSONAL BEHAVIOR

Objectives

At the completion of this chapter
you will be able to:

Describe how the five levels of human needs
influence your behavioral patterns

Prioritize your needs and minimize your wants

Perspective

Often we get confused in our attempts to sort out our needs versus our wants. It is important to note that our needs are at the origins of our behavior. Our thoughts influence two behaviors: 1) eliminate something that is not needed and 2) complete tasks that satisfy needs. We frequently miss our mark, because of our inability to follow through and successfully satisfy our needs that are tied to our values, goals, and standards. Moreover, we often do not identify with our need to establish values, set goals, and establish standards until we experience a life crisis. Take control of your health by living a healthy lifestyle. Understanding the difference between wants and needs are essential to your overall health and decision-making. Take care of your needs as a prerequisite of eliminating your wants. Make sure that your decisions relative to your personal behavior are embedded in sustainable health practices.

Needs

Needs are the essential elements for survival. It is important that we understand the essential needs required for mental, physical, and spiritual growth and development. I live my life by twelve jewels as my essential needs for survival. Those twelve jewels are: (1) knowledge (2) wisdom (3) understanding (4) freedom (5) justice (6) equality (7) food (8) clothing (9) shelter (10) love (11) peace and (12) happiness. Psychologist, Abraham Maslow, 1943; developed the five levels of human needs chart (Figure 1) that places emphasis on the psychological and the physical environment. One thing to note: the physical needs are more urgent and must be met before the psychological needs can be considered.

Physical Needs

Your physical needs include food, clothing, shelter, water, and warmth. When examining your physical needs, make certain that you identify with items that are necessary for good health and contribute to sustainable living. It is critical for you to carefully examine how you sustain your physical needs.

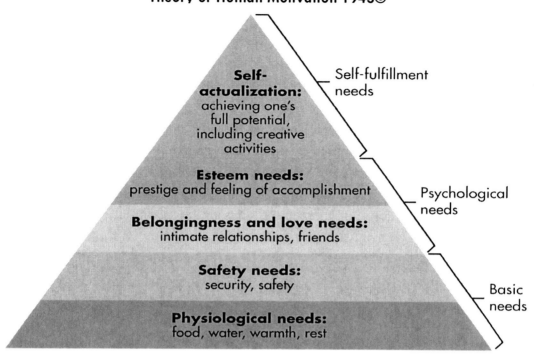

Figure 1: Maslow's Chart of Hierarchy Needs - Abraham Maslow. Theory of Human Motivation 1943©

Safety and Security

Danger should be considered a stranger in your life! Take heed when you hear phrases like, "you are in danger of failing," "UV rays from the sun can reach dangerous levels," and "not wearing your seat belt is not only unlawful but also dangerous." These phrases should signal or prompt you to take a different course of action and find a safe space. You need to feel safe and stay clear from any type of unbecoming behavior, irresponsible behavior, and any other behavior that hurts others as well. Fulfilling your security needs is based on your expectations of self and your environment. Constructing sound values, goals, and high standards will contribute to a daily repertoire of behavior and practices that add to your sense of safety and security.

Love and Acceptance

Warning! Love and acceptance are not always fair. More than ever, the need to feel or be loved has been pole vaulted to the top of the priority needs list for many school age kids. Everyone needs to know and experience the cradle of human affection. However, you should not expect to be loved by all people you encounter. Furthermore, it is critical for you to know that acceptance, support, praise, and love from others are predicated on your internal actions and behaviors, as well as your actions and behaviors towards others. Love can be dangerous, because it is a learned behavior built on prior experiences and interaction with and among family and friends. Whether good or bad, those actions and behaviors are correlated with your current and future actions and behaviors. The foundation of love and acceptance originates during infancy and the early childhood stages of life. It is essential for you to fully understand your origins of love and acceptance.

Know that your love and acceptance origins can positively impact your behaviors and actions. Understand that repeated behaviors that yield desired outcomes for you do not always equate to mutual feelings for the person(s) you are dealing with. Behaviors that do not yield favorable outcomes should NOT be repeated. It is critical for you to have input in your development. As you continue to learn and grow, you must continually engage in behaviors and actions that yield promise, and perhaps, a safe haven for gaining love and acceptance.

Esteem

One way to define or redefine your esteem is to have self-respect. It is dangerous to seek respect and admiration without having a sense of self. The key ingredient for obtaining and sustaining high self-esteem is to discover your true talent(s) and continuously work on developing self-confidence. Your esteem is important because when others around you sense that you have self-respect they interact with you with a great deal of admiration and exhibit similar behaviors.

Self-Actualization

Self-actualization is the highest level of Maslow's human needs theory. This is where you want to be. You will know that you have arrived here when you have an intrinsic need to reach your full potential. The need to work hard to be the best at what you do is a testament to you for aspiring to get better. You have arrived when your actions and behavior mirror that of your positive influences. These influences are part of your understanding of yourself and what you need to do to fulfill your goals. It's also what you need to travel the roads less traveled with a strong belief that you will reach your destination. Remember, life is a journey. Once you reach one destination, you have to saddle up and move on to reach your next goal.

NO EXCUSES!

Excuses are tools of the incompetent. They build monuments of nothing. Those who specialize in them seldom accomplish anything.

Some people are driven by rewards and recognition. Regardless of what you do in life, know that there will always be influence and motivation behind your decisions and behaviors. It is with deep conviction that I ask you to work on building and sustaining a foundation grounded with intrinsic motivation. People who have intrinsic motivation are self-motivated, and they succeed at things, because they possess internal desire. Intrinsic motivation is a good trait to have, because other people recognize when you are authentic about your words and actions.

I also caution you about receiving awards and recognition. There are only two types of awards a person can receive (1) objective award and (2) subjective award. If and when you receive an objective award be proud of your accomplishment. Objective awards have merit and criteria as variables to determine the recipient of the award. Subjective awards are given without merit and without considering substantiative criteria. You do not want to be on the receiving end of a subjective award. Subjective awards are somewhat political, are based on popularity, and are sometimes driven by agendas. Subjective awards can also be rescinded, revoked, or returned. Moreover, when you understand who you are, you will never be concerned about an award. Serving your purpose on earth will be of far greater importance than being recognized for it!

INVICTUS
William Ernest Henley (1849 – 1902)

Out of the night that covers me,
Black as a Pit from pole to pole,
I thank whatever gods may be
For my unconquerable soul.

In the fell clutch of circumstance
I have not winced nor cried aloud.
Under the bludgeonings of chance
My head is bloody, but unbowed.

Beyond this place of wrath and tears
Looms but the Horror of the shade,
And yet the menace of the years
Finds, and shall find me, unafraid.

It matters not how strait the Gate,
How charged with punishments the Scroll.
I am the Master of my fate:
I am the Captain of my soul.

 # My Personal and Suggested Readings and Instrumental Music Selections

READ

Blanchard, Ken. (1999). *The Heart of a Leader: Insights on the Art of Influence.* ColoradoSprings: Honor Books.

Cole, Edwin L. (2003). *The Power of Potential.* Southlake: Watercolor Books.

Comer, James P. (2008). *Waiting for a Miracle: Why Schools Can't Solve our Problems—and How We Can.* New York: PLUME.

Covey, Stephen R. (1989). *The 7 Habits of Highly Effective People.* New York: Fireside.

Greenleaf, Robert K. (2002). *Servant Leadership: A Journey into the Nature of Legitimate Power and Greatness:* Mahwah: Paulist Press.

Johnson, Spencer. (2002). *Who Moved My Cheese?* New York: Putnam.

Pinkney, Alphonso. (1984). *The Myth of Black Progress.* New York: Cambridge Press.

Poitier, Sidney. (2002). *The Measure of Man: A Spiritual Autobiography.* New York: HarperCollins.

LISTEN

Common; *Real People*

DJ Muggs vs. GZA-The Genius; *General Principles*

Groove Theory; *Keep Trying*

Jay Electronica; *Exhibit A*

Jean Grae; *Pardon You*

Miles Davis and John Coltrane; *Live New York*

Raekwon; *Masters of our Fate*

The Stylistics; *Children of the Night*

Wale; *Varsity Blues*

Xzhibit; *The Foundation*

Chapter 2 Action Item
How would you describe your behavior traits and influences?

Provide a detailed summary explanation of the influences on your actions within the context of your most and least desired behaviors. This summary should represent a performance profile in narrative form.

_____

_____

_____

_____

_____

_____

_____

_____

_____

_____

_____

_____

_____

_____

_____

_____

_____

_____

_____

_____

_____

_____

_____

_____

_____

_____

_____

_____

_____

_____

_____

_____

_____

_____

_____

_____

CHAPTER
3

CHOOSING TO BE RESILIENT: INTERNALIZE WHAT IS IMPORTANT TO YOU THEN SEEK HELP AND GUIDANCE

Objective

At the completion of this chapter
you will be able to:

Identify strategies to adjust to
or overcome trials and tribulations

Perspective

Mental Bondage is invisible violence.
– Dr. Asa Hilliard, Introduction to *Stolen Legacy* (1954)

To be resilient is to be able to adjust, recover, bounce back, and learn from difficult situations. Some people are more resilient than others. Resilient people are prepared for life's challenges and respond in healthy ways as issues arise. One may seek help and support from others including family members, friends and mentors. It is the resilient one who develops a laser-like focus, stays optimistic, and does not let tough times interfere with personal goals and dreams. One must examine the issue(s) and learn and grow from those experiences. Despite the many challenges that African American students often face in school, many are successful. Many are able to remain motivated and achieve academic excellence despite the circumstances (Catteral, 1998; Hale-Benson, 2001). However, the success that these children and adolescents exhibit amidst these challenges is frequently overlooked. Academic motivation is often at the bottom of the student's list of priorities. This reality is brought forth by persistent undesirable events such as: (a) limited financial resources, (b) parental stress and distress, and (c) lowered teacher/staff expectations (McLoyd, 1990). However, it should be noted that school leaders on the national level are now working with a sense of urgency to effectively utilize appropriated funding sources including Title I Funding, Race to the Top (RTTT) and School Improvement (SIG) Grants, to effectively address academic achievement for the resilient students who desire success. Furthermore, many gifted, accelerated, honors students, i.e., top-end (20 percent) of the class in these same schools are often ignored, because the majority of educational policy is driven to address the bottom-end (20 percent) of the students. It takes a special kind of school leader to be willing and able to move all students from at-risk to at-promise regardless of their socio-economic status.

Unimaginable outcomes for the most vulnerable students require
imaginable leadership.
– Rosa A. Smith (2005)

The existence of at least one caring person who is passionately focused on the child's outcomes despite the challenges—allows that child to do his or her best. Werner and Smith's (1982) longitudinal study, covering more than 40 years, found that a favorite teacher was among the most frequently cited positive role models in the lives of resilient children. These "turnaround" teachers were not just instructors for academic skills for the youngsters, but also a confident and positive role model for personal identification. Furthermore, the research of Noddings (1984) has articulated that a caring relationship with a teacher gives youth the motivation for wanting to succeed. Under any challenging circumstance, you must learn to take the necessary eight steps to be resilient. These eight steps to resilience are highlighted and explained under each subheading below.

1. **Tighten up your relationships with members of your family.**
   Staying connected to your family members gives you added strength and benefits during difficult times. Furthermore, staying connected to your family and having courageous conversations about challenges and issues can speed up the recovery time from a setback with minimal damage. Talk to your family about the good and bad things you experience.

2. **Establish and foster a close relationship with a mentor – become part of a mentorship program.**
   A mentor is a responsible person who will provide guidance and leadership. A typical mentor could be a coach, counselor, teacher, school administrator, aunt, uncle, relative, or any other responsible adult. It is important that you spend quality time with your mentor. It is your duty to discuss difficult situations, and to get suggestions when facing adversity, but most importantly, you MUST co-construct your mission, vision, and goals with your mentor and devise a success plan and stick to it.

3. **Choose associates who are supportive and who consistently exhibit responsible behavior.**
   To choose your friends wisely is to choose to succeed! It is important for you to choose friends who will encourage you to demonstrate responsible behavior during difficult times. Choose friends who will listen to you and respond appropriately. Stay away from individuals who behave in harmful ways.

4. **Do not avoid difficult situations.**
   Do not go into denial when difficult things happen. Face your fears ,and work through the challenges. Difficult things go away over time; invest your time in putting difficult situations to rest. You cannot fix what you cannot face.

5. **Do not engage in harmful behaviors as a coping mechanism for dealing with crisis.**
Addressing difficulty with anger and negative emotions only leads to more difficult situations. Irrational behavior, drinking, smoking, and violence are not the ways to cope with or fix your challenges. In fact, many of these mechanisms are diseases for which people receive long-term and short-term treatment. Work with your mentor or family to find helpful ways to cope with difficult situations.

6. **Seek support in all phases of your life, especially when you really need it.**
Reach out to the people you trust and ask for help when you are faced with trouble. Do not be afraid to ask for help regardless of how big or small your problem is.

7. **Discuss your issues with your parents and guardian(s).**
When and while overcoming adversity, it is important for you to establish a support group that will be honest and forthcoming. Never box yourself into a situation in which you feel like no one understands you or what you are going through. Your parents possess and sustain sober judgment and should provide the confidence that you need, especially in difficult times.

8. **Serve your school and community in extra-curricular and co-curricular activities.**
Being involved in extra-curricular activities and co-curricular activities is a critical way of feeling a sense of connection and staying connected. Your membership with any organization, club, or sports team provides a sense of belonging, but your level of participation determines your valor.

Success is uncommon, therefore not to be enjoyed by the common man.
I'm looking for uncommon people.
– Cal Stoll

NO EXCUSES!

Excuses are tools of the incompetent. They build monuments of nothing. Those who specialize in them seldom accomplish anything.

As a kid I never knew that I was poor economically because my vision and thoughts were rich and authentic. I did not understand the definition of poverty until I studied urban sociology in undergraduate school. You must understand all the elements around you; but moreover, your role in society is determined by how much you want to contribute to society. You will face many challenges in life. It is important that you know that there is no such thing as "things beyond your control." Once you understand who you are and know where you are going, you will control and dictate most things in your life. I took the approach that my income will not determine my outcome, but my outcome will determine my income.

 ## My Personal and Suggested Readings and Instrumental Music Selections

READ

Brown, Gilbert, O. (1994). *Debunking the Myth: Stories of African American University Students.* Bloomington: Phi Delta Kappa Educational Foundation.

Ladson-Billings, Gloria. (1994*). The Dreamkeepers: Successful Teachers of African American Children.* San Francisco: Jossey-Bass.

McNair, Carl S. (2011). *In the Spirit of Ronald E. McNair. Astronaut: An American Hero.* Atlanta: MAP.

Yeakey, Carol C. and Henderson, Ronald D. (2003). *Surmounting All Odds: Education, Opportunity, and Society in the New Millenium.* Greenwich: IAP.

LISTEN

Foreign Exchange; *Brave New World*

Nas; *The World is Yours*

Rick Ross Feat John Legend; *Magnificent*

Talib Kweli; *Everything Man*

Tammi Terrell; *I Cried*

9th Wonder; *Situations*

Chapter 3 Action Item
How would you describe personal resilience?

Provide a detailed summary explanation of a situation past or present where you have demonstrated personal resilience. This summary should represent a situation and action plan in narrative form.

CHAPTER
4

MENTAL SWAGGER: EXHIBIT SELF-CONFIDENCE, BE ASSERTIVE, AND BE VISIBLE

Don't worry if people are not listening to you;
worry that they are watching you.
– author unknown

Objectives

At the completion of this chapter
you will be able to:

Establish a living creed
and learn how to live by it

Exhibit confidence in your
thoughts, decisions, and actions

Perspective

You got it within you to succeed in life, to be happy and to be proud of yourself. No matter what anyone has told you, no matter what you believe right now, you've got it.
–Patricia Murphy; Educator, Ottawa, Canada (1996)

Many people have lost touch with their inner peace and beauty because of their loss of appetite for success. In today's society, it is no easy task to feel secure and display confidence when expressing your feelings, ideas, and thoughts. Many kids have lost that hunger primarily because of fear of failure and peer acceptance. This false premise is prevalent today, because many students do not posses their own definition of success. With that said, anyone and everyone can lend an opinion to determine if someone is considered a failure. Swagger, as we know it today, is the pop culture definition of self-confidence and assertiveness.

Walking the Talk: Taking the Necessary Steps to Appropriately Demonstrate Swagger

1. Ask these questions before taking action:
   Will my decisions please or disappoint my parents?
   Will my actions promote health and safety for myself and for others around me?
   Are my thoughts, decisions, and actions in accordance with the standards for ethical living, school policies and procedures, and with local, state, and federal laws and regulations?
   Will my decisions positively impact my character and reputation?
   Are my decisions reflective of what my parents/mentor teach me?
   Are my decisions parallel to the mission, vision, and goals of the family, club, sport, and/or organization I represent?

2. Establish a creed and live by it! Make special use of your creed when you are faced with something that opposes your belief system. Lean on your creed as a constant message and reminder that you are what you are in this world, but do not minimize yourself in the process.

3. When in doubt, calculate your risks after you talk with your parents and/or your mentor. Do not fall victim to the "man-up" hype. Many men do not man-up to a lot of things, primarily because many men need mentors

and coaches to help them learn to address their short-comings in life. Enjoy life and allow your swagger to serve as your confidence needle. Use a common sense approach to life and do not lose your identity in the process. Swagger does not mean that you have to portray something/someone you are not. Be confident, be assertive, and be smart. Use your abilities, and do what you set out to do. More importantly, have fun in the process.

NO EXCUSES!

Excuses are tools of the incompetent. They build monuments of nothing. Those who specialize in them seldom accomplish anything.

Contemplating Success?

Be optimistic! Be epic! See the outcome, but respect the process. A confident individual is one who begins with the end in mind. The confident person expects favorable outcomes as a result of his or her actions. The confident person believes that he or she can succeed at a specific activity and, more than likely, possesses a positive attitude throughout the process.

Whatever endeavor you choose, please make certain that you have a positive attitude and outlook for yourself. This kind of energy will permeate throughout your environment. People around you will feel your energy and enthusiasm. Furthermore, you will gain supporters to help you toward reaching your goals.

Self-Confidence?

Self-confidence is NOT accepting no for an answer. Self-confidence is growing up in the inner city with all the urban pathologies placed before you: single parent home, father not consistently in your life, mother and father did not complete high school, drugs, alcohol, and violence. These things contribute significantly to your community backdrop. Teenage pregnancy is rampant among your peers. Many of your male friends have been killed, incarcerated, or are addicted to drugs, but you look around and recommit your life to a different outcome and reach back and try to get others to the other side with you.

Self-confidence is a belief system that breeds success. Self-confidence is the ability to think on higher levels about your participation and success rates. Find your drive from within and make sure you bring it out. Do not be afraid of success. Fear is one of the biggest obstacles that human beings face, but it can also serve as a motivator. The first step to success is to face your fears. The second step to success is to know that swagger is 90 percent mental and 10 percent external. The external part is representative of your intellectual capital, which dictates how you look, walk, and act.

On Developing a Superior Mindset

I am here to tell you that it is ok, in fact, highly recommended that you develop a superior mindset. Dr. Carter G. Woodson said, "In the long run, there is not much discrimination against superior talent." Think about it in this context, Tiger Woods was ranked the number one golfer in the world for more than eleven years before dropping in the world rankings. Tiger had a laser-like focus, clarity, drive and concentration. Tiger possessed a singular intent, to beat the course not the opponents he faced. I challenge you to develop the superior mindset to prepare and exceed beyond adequate in anything that you do in life whether it's taking the ACT or SAT tests, or passing your driver's license examination. I challenge you to become your own free agent and achieve and fulfill your goals and dreams. Free agency cannot be a term only associated with sports. You have to develop a superior mindset and control your own destiny. I also caution you to prepare for the mental anguish that success breeds. Whether you win or lose you will be criticized, so you might as well prepare and develop the mindset to win. The late great Al Davis, owner and coach of the Oakland Raiders had three catch phrases that are still embedded in my brain: (1) commitment to excellence (2) you don't adjust, you dominate and (3) just win baby.

The will to win, the desire to succeed, the urge to reach your full potential are the keys that will unlock the door to personal and mental excellence.
– The late great Eddie Robinson
All-time winning football coach Grambling State University.

Vision is the art of seeing things invisible.
– Jonathan Swift

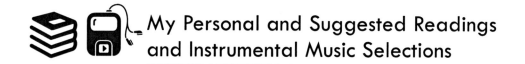

My Personal and Suggested Readings and Instrumental Music Selections

READ

Attab, Kaleem. (2005). *Lee, Spike: That's My Story and I'm Sticking to It.* New York: Norton & Company

Ellison, Ralph. (1980 renewed). *The Invisible Man.* New York: Vintage International.

Graham, Steadman (2004). *Move Without the Ball: Put Your Skills and Magic to Work for You.* New York: Fireside.

Jones, Reginald L. (1991). *Black Psychology.* Berkley: Cobb and Henry.

Koch, R. (2004). *Living The 80/20 Way: Work Less, Worry Less, Succeed More, Enjoy More.* Yarmouth: Nicholas Brealey.

Manus, A. (1999). *A Fire You Can't Put Out: The Civil Rights Life of Birmingham's Reverend Fred Shuttlesworth.* Tuscaloosa: University of Alabama

Noguera, Pedro, A. (2008). *The Trouble with Black Boys…And other Reflections on Race, Equity, and the Future of Public Education.* San Francisco: Jossey-Bass.

LISTEN

Black Star; *KOS-Knowledge of Self*

Diana Ross; *Ain't No Mountain High Enough*

GZA; *Publicity*

Jay-Z; *What More Can I Say?*

Lupe Fiasco; *Kick, Push*

Mano D; *All My Eyes Can See*

Miles Davis; *So What*

Pete Rock; *Take Your Time*

Pharoahe Monch; *The Truth*

Tribe Called Quest; *Get A Hold*

Chapter 4 Action Item
Describe your swagger?

Provide a detailed summary explanation of your swagger in the context of self-confidence. This summary should represent your swagger profile that represents your confidence action plan in narrative form.

_____
_____
_____
_____
_____
_____
_____
_____
_____
_____
_____
_____
_____
_____
_____
_____
_____
_____
_____
_____
_____
_____
_____
_____
_____
_____
_____
_____
_____
_____
_____
_____
_____
_____
_____
_____
_____
_____
_____

CHAPTER
5

COMMUNICATION SKILLS: HOW YOU DRESS IS HOW YOU WILL BE ADDRESSED

Clothes and manners do not make the man,
but where he is made they greatly improve his appearance.
– Arthur Ashe, Professional Tennis Player

Objectives

At the completion of this
chapter you will be able to:

Improve your image and physical traits

Protect your personal brand

Understand the importance
of being well-groomed

Dress appropriately for specific occasions

Perspective

Healthy relationships are determined by how well you communicate. Communication is the method in which a message is delivered, received, processed, and understood. For the purpose of this chapter, our focus is triangulated in that we will address a few elements of nonverbal communication: your appearance, your actions, and your body language. The way you look, dress, act, and respond will determine your fate on many levels.

He who possesses the power of language will not be a hapless victim.
– author unknown

Appearance

Your first impression is a lasting impression. Your appearance sends a strong message that will garner a response—either positive or negative. People create a category for you based on how you present yourself. Your appearance determines preliminary credibility of who you are as an individual and to what extent you will engage in meaningful dialogue with others you encounter. Make no mistake, people have prejudices about certain standards of appearance. However, your standard appearance should be that of one who is clean, neat, well-groomed, and well-dressed. The focus is not about how much your clothes cost, but how well you put yourself together. Your overall appearance tells others how you feel about yourself. It is known that people generally respond more favorably to individuals whose appearance is presentable and, more importantly, respectable.

Discretion is more important than articulation.
– author unknown

Actions

More than anything else, your manners are an essential part of how you verbally communicate with others. Manners are vital and they guide proper behavior. Using good manners sends the message that you want others around you to relax and feel comfortable. Using proper manners is a common-sense approach to facilitate reciprocal behaviors that speak to being kind and respectable. The chief language spoken in Manners 101 makes use of words like *please, excuse me, pardon me, thank you,* and *may I.* These actions demonstrate courtesy as well as respect and care for a person's feelings. Writing your teacher or someone who has helped you a note of thanks or a card to show your appreciation reflects your thoughtfulness. This action speaks to your character and demonstrates that you are considerate to others.

Body Language

It is imperative that you understand the implications of your body language. Your appearance may be top notch, but if your body language does not match your appearance you could experience an unpleasant outcome from your encounter with others. Your body language is just that, another language in which we communicate subconsciously with our body movements, facial expressions, gestures, and posture, sending messages to others. Although you are not using words, your messages are succinctly conveyed to others. For example, your facial expression will send a clear message of your mood prior to speaking to anyone. One of the guiding principles of Harris Enterprise International, LLC is: "Professionalism starts with a smile, collaboration ends with a wow!" Other favorable ways to communicate using body language include but are not limited to: 1) a firm hand shake and 2) a wink and nodding of the head conveying "I agree." When you engage in dialogue with others, please exhibit good posture at all times. Even if you disagree with someone be respectful by keeping your posture intact. Pay close attention to your body language at all times. Body language is a universal language that allows you to pick up on clues to interpret messages of other people. Body language can also be used to reinforce and make your spoken words more concise and more effective. In addition, pay close attention to your personal space as you communicate with others. Always think of every situation as a comfortable situation and keep your personal space intact and respect the space of others at all times.

Dress for Success

Good grooming includes choosing appropriate clothing and caring for the clothes that you have. If you want to dress for success, follow these four essential elements:

1. Wear clothes that match your personal brand. Your clothing style should convey your personality. Develop a personal clothing style that helps you look sharp and convey confidence. Avoid wearing loud colors to job interviews or business events. Wear the appropriate clothes that match the occasion.

2. Wear clothing that fits properly and fits your budget. Try on clothes before you buy them. It is always wise to ask the sales associate what he/she thinks of the fit. Choose clothing that is not too long, loose, big, short, or tight. It is never appropriate to sag your pants. Wear your belt appropriately and at all times. Ensure that your shoes fit properly as well. You should invest in at least two suits, white shirts/blouses, a few neck ties or bow ties as appropriate, and a pair of black or brown dress shoes. Determine your budget, and do not overspend on your clothing. Lastly, do not be overly impressed with designer labels.

3. Wear clothes that are clean and neat. Follow instructions on how to care for your clothes (hand wash, machine wash, tumble dry, or dry clean). Of course, always adhere to the golden rule, and wear clean underwear and socks every day.

4. Wear clothes that are appropriate for the situation. Use discretion; however, it is my recommendation that you wear a suit to any interview, presentation, or formal/social event. Wear business casual attire when instructed to do so. You should be clean and neat everyday you attend school, work, or an event.

NO EXCUSES!

Excuses are tools of the incompetent. They build monuments of nothing. Those who specialize in them seldom accomplish anything.

Dress neat, wear the appropriate clothes for every occasion, tuck your shirt in your pants, wear your pants above your waistline, and use language appropriately. The definition of sanity: practice the above ritual over and over and over and you will get the same results!

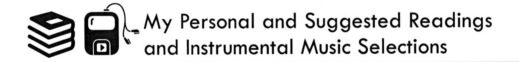 **My Personal and Suggested Readings and Instrumental Music Selections**

READ

Bixler, Susan & Nix-Rice, Nancy. *The New Professional Image: From Business Casual to the Ultimate Power Look-How to Tailor Your Appearance for Success in Today's Workplace.* Avon, MA: Adams Media Corporation. 1997

Carson, Reginald. (2011). *Stylistocrat.com.* Stylistocrat by R&R: America's Premier Fashion Stylists.

Flusser, Alan, (2002). *Dressing the Man: Mastering the Art of Permanent Fashion.* New York: HarperCollins.

Chapter 5 Action Item
How do you define Communication?

Provide a detailed summary explanation of how you dress and present yourself to the public. This summary should represent your actions and reactions to how others addressed you based upon how you were dressed in narrative form.

CHAPTER 6

LEADERSHIP AND MENTORING

This is no time to engage in the luxury of cooling off or to take the tranquilizing drug of gradualism. Now is the time to make real the promises of democracy.
– Dr. Martin Luther King, Jr., *I Have a Dream* (1963)

Objectives

At the completion of this chapter
you will be able to:

Identify different types of leaders

Identify leadership behaviors

Describe effective leadership traits

Identify national mentoring programs
and tell the purpose of each

Perspective

At some point in your life, you will likely become a member of a number of organizations. These organizations may include chess clubs, beta clubs, choirs, sports teams, scouts, fraternal organizations, mentoring organizations, singing groups, drum corps, and community associations. Each member of the organization can have an impact on the success of the mission, vision, goals and activities of the organization. It is critical that you start the internal process of learning how to work well with others. This will allow you to contribute to the overall effectiveness of the organization. Within every organization you have leaders and followers. Leaders are the individuals who have the power to influence the behavior of others. When you look at successful businesses, successful sports teams, successful schools and other successful organizations, you find that they have one thing in common—great leadership! It is critical that you enlist the services of a mentor or become part of a mentoring program that has all the essential components that are parallel to your values and could assist you in reaching your goals and objectives.

He who has never learned to obey can never be a commander.
– Aristotle

Many organizations do not recruit, but they work with individuals who seek to become a better person by contributing to the established foundation of the organization while learning to enhance their personal characteristics while working collectively with all members of the organization. The significance of this commentary relative to leadership behavior cannot be overstated. Therefore, working on their own ability to lead effectively and model desirable behaviors, **students** (you) must adopt and embody those qualities that influence the actions of their peers, parents, mentors, teachers, administrators, and community stakeholders. Leadership should be defined broadly as a social process in which a member of a group or organization influences the interpretation of internal and external events, the choice of goals or desired outcomes, the organizing of work activities, individual motivation and abilities, power relations, and shared orientations (Yukl, 1998). Senge (1990) defines leadership as the capability of a group of people to shape its future and maintain the significant processes of change necessary to do so.

Different Types of Leaders

(1) Transformational Leader

The transformational leader is able to transform commitment levels of those around him by being the example of what he expects from all individuals in the organization. He has deep conviction about their goals, is determined to execute, and takes risks against conventional wisdom.

(2) Visionary Leader

The visionary leader captures the collective dreams of awesome things to come. She elevates ambition.

(3) Constructivist Leader

The constructivist leader provides leaders at all levels with a conceptual framework for leadership that is defined as reciprocal and purposeful within the organization. The constructivist leader draws on the knowledge that the individuals within the organization already possess.

Leadership Behaviors

1. **Take Risks.** A leader must take risks with the understanding of what opportunities exist or can be created. Moreover, a leader must be able to produce results. Taking risks allows a leader to capitalize on windows of current and future success opportunities. Taking risks shifts the paradigm to doing things to improve yourself and others around you through exposure to new situations.

2. **Impose Your Will.** Whenever an opportunity presents itself a leader must impose his or her will to succeed. The leader's primary responsibility is to resist distractions and concentrate on what matters most. Be clear with one's self, others, and the overall goals and values. Stay on purpose.

3. **Be Impeccable with your Word.** Be enthusiastic about what you say and what you are doing! A leader's success lies within his or her ability to convey deep personal convictions to others. Possessing a clear mission and vision of what you aim to achieve will help guide your decisions, inspire people to follow you, overcome adversity, alleviate uncertainty, and give you the courage to stand and deliver. A leader must stand on his/her belief system and build confidence in the people who support them. Never waive your integrity!

4. **Construct Movement.** A leader must generate movement by transforming

knowledge into action. She must influence people to channel their energies into constructive thinking for appropriate activities. She must mobilize a unified workforce and create a culture that speaks to development and harmonious movement toward the mission and vision of the organization.

5. **Accept Responsibility.** Leaders do not rest on their laurels or on the efforts of past successes. They must be prepared for the next initiative with an action plan ready for collaborative discussion. They must get out in front of the curve and be prepared to address the latest trends, statistics, and pathologies that they are presented with from research findings and statistical analysis. When the organization does not meet its goals, the leader must accept responsibility and be accountable for the shortfall. However, the leader must be able to assess the outcome and regroup with an adjustment plan of action and then proceed with the mission.

As an emerging leader, there are five practical traits that you need to master:

1. **Know how to conduct and lead a meeting.** It is imperative that you are well versed on parliamentary procedure.

2. **Set an example.** Be the example of how you want your followers to act, work, and behave. Exhibit high moral and ethical standards at all times

3. **Motivate Followers.** Understand the difference between intrinsic motivation and extrinsic motivation. Use these two forms of motivation to move the individuals within your organization to move accordingly. *Intrinsic motivation* is based on taking pleasure in an activity rather than working towards an external reward. It is driven by an interest or enjoyment in the task itself, and exists from within as opposed to anything external. *Extrinsic motivation* is when a person is motivated by external factors, as opposed to the internal drivers. Extrinsic motivation drives people to do things for tangible rewards or pressures, rather than for the joy of it.

4. **Use Tact.** Always know what to do and say at all times; especially when certain things are sensitive in nature but need your endorsement.

5. **Give Recognition.** Praising people often brings out the best in their work. Praise people honestly to show your appreciation. Follow the simple rule: reprimand privately and praise publicly.

Choosing an Effective Mentoring Program

People join organizations for various reasons. Some organizations have specific criteria in place as prerequisites for membership. In many cases, people join organizations to be part of something that they have identified with such as the mission, vision, or principles of the organization. The purpose for mentoring programs is to help prepare young people for leadership roles in the future. Everyone, no matter their age, should have a mentor or be part of an organization that provides on-going mentoring and fellowship. When seeking membership you must ask these questions:

1. What value can I bring to the organization/mentoring program?

2. Will the mentors within this program help me and others attain our individual and collective goals?

3. Will I enjoy being part of the mentoring program?

4. What makes this mentoring program different from others?

5. Who are the adults in this mentoring program? Are they successful professionals? What types of adversity have they faced and overcome?

6. Will the mentoring program provide opportunities for the mentees to get exposure in their career path?

Mentoring is the process that involves formal and informal communication between the mentor and the mentee. It is relationship based. Mentorship is built on the premise that personal development takes form when a more experienced or more knowledgeable person helps a less experienced or less knowledgeable person. Organizations implement mentoring programs for various reasons and purposes. Some reasons include:

1. Helping young people develop and reach their full potential

2. Helping young people develop critical thinking skills necessary for success and survival

3. Helping to accelerate a young person's education and career path

4. Improving a young person's personal efficiency

See the list of some the nation's leading mentoring programs (Table 1). Furthermore, research the mentoring programs in your local community and state to see if the services being offered match your beliefs and can help you reach your goals.

Table 1: National Mentoring Programs	
Omega Psi Phi Fraternity, Inc. Delta Mu Mu Chapter *Black Rhinos Mentoring Program* **Contact:** **Patrick Tolbert, Basileus** **P.O. Box 88097** **Atlanta, GA 30336** **pctolbert@bellsouth.net** **krs@dmmomegas.org**	The basic premise of the Black Rhinos Mentoring program is to *Uplift* young African-American males to their fullest potential. We have recognized that there is a need in the North Atlanta area for young men to interact with positive African American male role models. Representative members of the Delta Mu Mu chapter of Omega Psi Phi Fraternity, Inc. serve as mentors and role models for the students who become part of the program. The black rhinoceros was recently declared extinct due to continued poaching and lack of conservation. Similarly, according to educational and statistical research, it could be said that educated, upwardly mobile, tax-paying African-American males are also becoming an endangered species. We are convinced that with proper leadership and a collection of the appropriate influences, these factors of urban life can be enhanced. Members of our beloved Delta Mu Mu chapter of Omega Psi Phi Fraternity, Inc., consist of community leaders and individuals with practical experiences and relative ties to admonishing the issues that plague our youth. The young men will have the opportunity to interact with clergymen, pediatricians, economists, educators, demographers, lawyers, nutritionists, urban planners, criminal justice officials, medical doctors, dentists, engineers, surgeons, executive level Fortune 500 leaders, real estate brokers, senior level financial advisors, and other professional members who represent this chapter of the Omega Psi Phi Fraternity, Inc. The Black Rhinos Mentoring Program will serve as a resource for students to learn, master, and sustain the skills needed for mainstream society, so that they can be economically viable and contribute to the creative development of self and their immediate and global community.
100 Black Men of America **Mentoring the 100 Way®** **Dr. Howard Rasheed** **220 Brascote Lane** **Wilmington, NC 28412** **Phone: 910.431.1233** **Email: hrasheed@ec.rr.com** **Email: info@100blackmen.org**	A holistic mentoring program that addresses the social, emotional and cultural needs of children ages 8-18. Members of the 100 are trained and certified to become mentors, advocates, and role models for the youth within their communities. Through chapter operated one-on-one and group mentoring efforts, our members forge relationships that positively impact our greatest resource, our youth. The program focuses on building essential skills needed to become productive, contributing citizens.

Call Me MISTER Contact: **Call Me MISTER** **203 Holtzendorff** **Clemson University** **Clemson, SC 29634** Phone: Toll-free: 1-800-640-2657 E-mail: MISTER@clemson.edu	The mission of the Call Me MISTER (acronym for Mentors Instructing Students Toward Effective Role Models) initiative is to increase the pool of available teachers from a broader more diverse background, particularly among the state's lowest performing elementary schools. Student participants are largely selected from among under-served, socio-economically disadvantaged and educationally at-risk communities. The Call Me MISTER program is contributing to the talent pool of excellent teachers by identifying and supporting students who are literally "touching the future" by teaching children.
The National Rights of Passage Institute **Cleveland, OH** **Contact: Paul Hill** **2749 Woodhill Road** **Cleveland, OH 44104** **Phone: (216) 707-6030** **Fax: (216) 791-9754** Email: nropi@aol.com	Rites of Passage, as a developmental and transformational process, are culturally-specific, not universal. It is based on the multi-cultural premise that a group must recognize and affirm itself before it is able to share and appreciate the differences of others. Rites of Passage as a process also recognizes that entry into adult life involves the realization of social obligations and the assumption of responsibility for meeting them. Initiation sets a time on the journey for bringing the individuals into formal and explicit relation with their kindred. It also confronts them with some of their basic social ties, reaffirms them and thus makes obvious to them their status against the days when they will have to adopt them in earnest. Rites of Passage as a developmental and transformational process will not only provide self-development and cultural awareness, but also will foster a sense of belonging. Adolescents and adults will become part of community life, not persons alone, lacking support, sanction, and purpose.
McNair Achievement Programs (MAP) **Contact: Dr. Carl S. McNair** **President and CEO** **The McNair Achievement Program** **Telphpone:404-346-3262** info@mcnairachievement.com	The McNair Achievement Programs have developed and implemented successful educational programs that promote academic excellence and personal achievement. These programs are also designed to inspire and empower individuals to pursue their goals and dreams. Annually, Dr. Carl McNair conducts educational seminars and delivers keynote speeches to numerous organizations and Trio programs; this includes over 100 colleges and universities with McNair Scholars Programs, Upward Bound, Talent Search and/or other educational programs. Carl is also Founder and President Emeritus of the Dr. Ronald E. McNair Foundation. The foundation was established in honor of his brother, Dr. Ronald E. McNair, who perished along with six of his astronaut colleagues aboard the space shuttle Challenger on January 28, 1986.

Beacon House Contact: Executive Director 601 Edgewood St., N.E., Suite 15 Washington, D.C. 20017 Phone: 202.529.7376 SErd@beaconhousedc.org	The College Bound Academic Mentoring Program matches students with college-educated volunteers to strengthen the student's math, language arts, and social skills while preparing them for the college journey. **S.T.R.I.D.E.** is dedicated to supporting and motivating youth towards *S*elf–awareness, *T*eam-work, *R*esponsibility, *I*ndependence, *D*iligence, and *E*xcellence, by nurturing talent and creativity through fashion oriented enrichment activities and productions, emphasizing leadership and advocacy, health and grooming, and etiquette.
Steve Harvey Mentoring Weekend For Young Men Contact: Elisha Silvera The Steve Harvey Foundation P.O. Box 52817 Atlanta, GA 30355	The Steve Harvey Mentoring Weekend for Young Men is a 4-day, 3-night program designed to teach the principles of manhood to young men to enable them to achieve their dreams and therefore become better men who are emotionally, politically and economically strong. Approximately one hundred young men, in grades 8-11, from around the country, will be pre-selected to travel to Dallas, TX with a parent or guardian for a weekend of mentoring. The program promotes life skills that will make a lasting impression on the lives of young men we serve.
Pearls of Wisdom Contact: Gerald Barber Shreveport, LA pearlsofwisdomgolf@yahoo.com Phone: 404.921.4488	The Pearls of Wisdom Program is an African American male/female golf and mentoring program, which fosters mental growth, academic achievement, golf playing skills, and college entrance for the students in the program. The primary goal of the program is to increase the matriculation rates of African American males and females entering college on golf scholarships and increase the participation rates of African American males and females on the PGA and WPGA tours.
Man-to-Man Mentoring Program Contact: Ernest Harvey Warner Robbins Middle School phone: 229.938.3756 ernest.harvey@hcbe.net	The Man-to-Man Mentoring program at Warner Robbins Middle School has been providing a full-service mentoring model for the last seven years. Located in Houston County, GA, the program is multifaceted and serves Black, White, Hispanic, Mexican, gifted, advanced, behaviorally challenged, and Level 1 students. WRMS is a title 1 school where nearly 70% of the student population receives free and reduced meals. Many of the students fall in the "at risk" category. Man-to-Man is built on the Motto: "No Excuses" and is structured to facilitate and support the *each-one-teach-one* methodology via peer mentoring and peer role models. The aim of Man-to-Man Mentoring program is that the young men take ownership of their actions (positive or negative), help build esteem, guide students to academic stability and mold good citizens. Our curriculum is based upon modules and thematic units on life skills, respect for self and others, etiquette, manners, self-determination, conflict resolution and interpersonal skills needed for success in life.

London's Bridge Foundation Contact: Joe Briggs, Esq. jbriggs@londonsbridge.org London's Bridge P.O. Box 28502 Cleveland, Ohio 44182	The London's Bridge Foundation, founded in 2003, is an Ohio based non-profit corporation. Under the direction of London Fletcher, The London's Bridge Foundation is "building a bridge to our future" by addressing the inequities facing underprivileged and underrepresented children. Through our mentoring and charitable giving programs we teach boys and girls essential life skills and lessons. Specifically, London's Bridge builds standards of education, leadership, teamwork, and recreation while instilling values of volunteerism and philanthropy. The London's Bridge Foundation is a safe haven and refuge for our children.
Troupe21 & Associates Contact: Guy Troupe 509 Elm Street, Suite 306 Dallas, TX 75202 Phone: 214 749-7833 troupe21@troupe21.com	Troupe21 & Associates, LLC (Troupe21) is a Dallas, Texas-based human resources development company that specializes in providing customized and cost-effective products and services for athletic organizations, teams and corporations. We create cutting-edge solutions for our clients through abstracting, which involves summarizing and converting real-world events or ideas into models. Troupe21 is unique in its use of athletic research, paradigms, and techniques to create long-lasting individual and organizational memory.

What a man dislikes in his superiors,
let him not display in treatment to his subordinates.
– Tsing Sin

Risk Management:
A Personal Critique of the Unintended Consequences of Pseudo-Activism

The dangers of mentoring? Be careful with the interaction and language of the mentors and the mentoring programs as a whole. Avoid being associated with mentors and mentoring programs that utilize practices and phrases like, man-up. It is very difficult for adult men to carry out some of the most basic responsibilities as men. I will elaborate on this topic extensively in the forthcoming book: *Existential Thoughts – Postmodern Actions: Overstanding the Elements and Epistemology of the Education System in the Urban Terrain.* However, I must note that many of our male youth do not know how to be young men, because of the multiple layers of pressure associated with carrying the burdens of a man. Boys will be boys, but it is up to the adults to help facilitate the successful transitions from boyhood to manhood. To give a male youth the directive to Man-

Up is dangerous, because he will respond accordingly with social behaviors that are demonstrated in his immediate environment. Often times, these behaviors do not yield successful outcomes. In particular, when you look at the statistics of the African American youth and young adult incarceration, unemployment, and death rates, we cannot afford to spark someone's curiosity of taking actions of a man, especially when poor examples have been demonstrated across the board.

When I speak to groups of students in assembly settings, or any other group setting, I thoroughly observe them to get a preliminary read on their self-perceptions and their behaviors. Prior to the age of 15, many of our youth have experienced all the things that legal adults have experienced. We have too many issues today with our youth thinking they are adults. You cannot put this Man-Up logic in a different context and think it will be okay for our youth to function from that deficit model. Prison cannot be the place where you think about reforming individuals. Reform starts with you! Until you change you cannot expect anything around you to change. Institutions are defined by the DNA, mission, values, norms, traditions, ideals, and most importantly the people who represent them. No matter if it is Howard University or Harvard University; Apple Computers or TV/Radio One; Pepsi or Coca Cola; Microsoft, CNN, or Telemundo; Delta or Southwest; or even Yale or Jail—these institutions attract people with like minds and long-term aspirations.

Decide where you want to go now so that you do not have to pay a high price to get there. Remember, prison will accept you without any prerequisites. You do not need to produce reference letters, nor do you need a high school diploma.

Moreover, the prison system takes full advantage of poor test scores as early as 4th grade to forecast revenue. Some of the most intellectual men of our society pace the floors of our prisons. It is unfortunate that many of these men had to go to prison to realize their intellectual capital. As a result, they become intellectual property of a failing but lucrative system. Man-Up is just another adjective that describes the prisoner who fights for his survival daily.

We have a bad economy partly because we do not produce people who can contribute to the economy. Many people cannot contribute to the economy, because we have not contributed to their education. The prison industry has redefined the meaning of Gross Domestic Product (GDP). It is a gross reality to see the overrepresentation of African American males incarcerated and placed in special education classes. Check the statistical data (longitudinal data) on inmate and special education growth for African Americans since 1980. From 1980 to 1992, the African American incarceration rate increased by an average of 138.4 per 100,000 per year.

Still, despite a more than doubling of the African American incarceration rate in the 12 years prior to President Clinton's term in office, the African American incarceration rate continued to increase by an average rate of 100.4 per 100,000 per year. In total, between 1980 and 1999, the incarceration rate for African Americans more than tripled from 1156 per 100,000 to 3,620 per 100,000.
– Justice Policy Institute, 2001

You must fix and sustain a system of self. Until then you will contribute to or help create other elements of the current broken systems that exist today; **family system** – single parent households/poverty, **school system** – alarming dropout and failure rates, **judicial system** – growing population of inmates based upon legal technicalities.

Positive exposure and changes in social, cultural, and intellectual capital will bring about positive changes in behavior and norms relative to ethics, morals, and values for the individual who desires to live a healthy and quality life.

NO EXCUSES!

Excuses are tools of the incompetent. They build monuments of nothing. Those who specialize in them seldom accomplish anything.

Non-negotiable: every reader must become a mentee, mentor, or both. No exceptions because this is the only rule to the game of life. You must be willing to be helped and you must be willing to help others.

We need workers, not leaders.
Such workers will solve the problems which race leaders talk about.
– Dr. Carter G. Woodson

My Personal and Suggested Readings and Instrumental Music Selections

READ

Akbar, Na'im. (1991). *Visions for Black Men.* Tallahassee: Mind Productions & Associates, Inc.

Balch, T. J. and Robert, H. M. (2004). *Robert's Rules of Order in Brief: The Simple Outline of the Rules Most Often Needed at a Meeting, According to the Standard Authoritative Parliamentary Manual*, Revised Edition

Dortch, Jr., Thomas and 100 Black Men of America, Inc. (2000).*The Miracles of Mentoring: How to Encourage and Lead Future Generations.* New York: Doubleday Broadway Publishing Group.

Finzel, Hans. (1994). *The Top Ten Mistakes Leaders Make.* Colorado Springs: NexGen-Cook Communication Ministries.

Freire, Paulo. (1997). *Mentoring the Mentor, A Critical Dialogue with Paulo Freire.* NewYork: Peter Lang Publishing, Inc.

Harari, Oren. (2002). The Leadership Secrets of Colin Powell. New York: McGraw-Hill

Maxwell, John C. (1993). *Developing the Leader Within You.* Nashville: Thomas Nelson, Inc.

Mincy, Ronald B. (1994). *Nurturing Young Black Males.* Washington, DC: The Urban Institute

Thomas, David A. and Gabarro, John J. (1999). *Breaking Through: The Making of Minority Executives in Corporate America.* Boston: Harvard Business Review

LISTEN

Earth, Wind, & Fire; *Keep Your Head to the Sky*

Tribe Called Quest; *Lyrics to Go*

The ROOTS featuring Erykah Badu; *You Got Me*

Wes Montgomery; *The Art of Wes Montgomery*

9th Wonder; *Alright*

Chapter 6 Action Item
How do you describe Leadership and Mentoring?

Provide a detailed summary explanation of leadership and mentoring. This summary should represent a thorough explanation of leadership and mentoring in action. Provide a narrative form of your work and responses.

_____
_____
_____
_____
_____
_____
_____
_____
_____
_____
_____
_____
_____
_____
_____
_____
_____
_____
_____
_____
_____
_____
_____
_____
_____
_____
_____
_____
_____
_____
_____
_____
_____
_____
_____
_____
_____
_____

CHAPTER 7

CHOOSE YOUR BATTLES: THINK METHODICALLY, MAKE YOUR DECISIONS, AND THEN FIGHT!

You're either part of the problem or part of the solution.
–Eldridge Cleaver, (1968)

Objectives

At the completion of this chapter
you will be able to:

Understand how to critically think through the
problem solving process

Learn how to process information and make
informed decisions

Understand how your values, standards, and
goals impact the decision you make

Perspective

The beauty of life is that you must solve problems and make decisions that often impact, as well as determine your standard of living. The art of *choosing your battles* can eliminate ninety percent of your struggles. You must learn the all important skill of *making decisions.* Once learned and mastered, these two skill sets, solving problems and making decisions, can help you navigate through life's day-to-day challenges with confidence and enthusiasm, knowing that you will persevere.

Children attend school culturally embedded in their values and belief systems, appropriated from their immediate life experiences (Boykin, in press-b). However, schools are not neutral. Critical studies in the area of sociology of education (Apple, 1995; Giroux, 1983) hold that schools are "contested terrains," crucial arenas in which the struggle over ideas, values, and power in society are acted out. Schools are key institutions in which the knowledge of those who hold economic and social power is transmitted and legitimized (Apple, 1995). Knowledge and dispositions or cultural capital of dominant groups is rewarded while that of subordinated groups is negated (Bourdieu, 1977). Through differential distribution of knowledge and skills, schools socialize and sort students for unequal positions within the social division of labor, thus helping to reproduce social inequality (Oakes, 1985). Schools legitimize inequality along the lines of class, race, ethnicity, and gender.

You MUST take proactive steps to make informed decisions that have merit and sustainability What is a decision? How do I make decisions? A decision is simply an outcome to a response to a question, issue, problem, or a challenge. Be careful NOT to make decisions without thinking critically. Sometimes we make decisions on impulse. These decisions are often constructed due to your environment, experiences, and other influences. Understand that there are pros and cons in every decision that you make.

The Decision-Making Matrix

The Decision-Making Matrix (Table 2) demonstrates the step-by-step approach to making informed decisions that produces actions that are in accordance with the standards of ethical and moral living, show respect for self and others, follow parental and mentor expectations and guidelines, adhere to local, state, and federal rules, laws, policies and procedures, and promote sustainability with respect to good health, safety, and wellness.

Table 2 The Decision-Making Matrix

1. Identify the problem, issue, or challenge that requires a decision. Record your problem, issue, or challenge on paper and document all the information that led to the current situation. This exercise will allow you to see the situation more clearly.

2. Establish your goals and possible outcomes Construct a list of possible decisions based on short-term and long-term goals and how these decisions are aligned with your values, standards, and morals.

3. Involve your parent(s) and your mentor in the decision-making process. Never go alone when facing your problems, issues, and challenges. Allow your parents and mentor to assist you with solving problems and making decisions. The responsible adults can assist you by elaborating on the consequences of your thoughts and possible decisions. Consider the wisdom that comes with age from these adults who may have experienced similar problems, issues, and challenges. Solicit and consider their input with sincerity.

4. Ask questions to evaluate the pros and cons of your decision Make certain that your decisions are based on objectivity and NOT subjectivity.

5. Make decisions that are appropriate and sustainable How will my decisions impact my future, my family, my health, the current and future state of affairs for others? How will my decisions impact my character, values, standards, and morals?

6. Analyze and evaluate the outcome of your decision Make your decisions with intelligence. Look at the outcome of your decisions and carefully evaluate the progress. You must ask yourself: Did my decision meet my expected goal? Did my decision solve the problem, issue, or challenge? Record the pros and cons of your decisions, and more importantly, learn from your mistakes in the event a similar problem, issue, or challenge arises.

NO EXCUSES!

*Excuses are tools of the incompetent. They build monuments of nothing.
Those who specialize in them seldom accomplish anything.*

Many people talk about their problems, but do not address their problems. At some point you must decide if you are going to fix your problems or continue to live your life undecided.

 ## My Personal and Suggested Readings and Instrumental Music Selections

READ

Bach, David. (2005). *Start late Finish Early: A No-Fail Plan for Achieving Financial Freedom at Any Age.* New York: Broadway Books

Brunious, Loretta, J. (1998). *Constructing Sociality: Self-Portraits of Black Children Living in Poverty.* New York: Routledge.

Cleary, Thomas. (1988). *The Art of War: Sun Tzu.* Boston: Shambhala publications, Inc.

Edleman, Marian W. (2005). *I Can Make A Difference: A Treasury to Inspire Our Children.* New York: HarperCollins.

Hargreaves, A. and Fullan, M. (1998). *What's Worth Fighting For Out There?* New York: Teachers College Press.

NoGuera, Pedro. (2003). *City Schools and the American Dream: Reclaiming the Promise of Public Education.* New York: Teachers College Press.

LISTEN

De La Soul; *The Stakes Is High*

Gang Star; *Moment of Truth*

Goodie Mob; *Refuse Limitations*

Goodie Mob; *Sky High*

Jeezy; *Go Crazy*

Julie Dexter; *How Long*

9th Wonder; *Close Your Eyes*

Chapter 7 Action Item
What is your process on Choosing Your Battles?

Provide a detailed summary explanation on how you decide what is worth fighting for. This summary should represent a detailed explanation of your process on making decisions and your methodology on defending your actions in narrative form.

CHAPTER
8

KNOW AND UNDERSTAND YOUR LEARNING STYLE

When I stepped into my first college class
the first person I met was myself.
– Kevin Harris, Ed. D.

Objectives

At the completion of this chapter
you will be able to:

Understand all the elements of the
different learning styles

Understand the impact of your
personal learning style

Work toward reaching the mastery level by
effectively utilizing your learning style

Perspective

Leaders in urban schools may set the stage for children to absorb successful approaches to learning which link to positive academic outcomes. Thomas (2000) contends that successful implementation of the learner-centered approach is a promising method for raising the achievement levels of all students. McCombs and Whistler (1997) describe the learner-centered approach as:

> *...a dual focus that informs and drives educational decision-making with respect to the learners personal experiences, backgrounds, talents, interests, capacities, heredity, and needs in concert with the best available knowledge; and about learning how the most effective teaching practices promote the highest levels of motivation, learning, and achievement for all learners.*

The learner-centered approach was constructed to help students understand, confront, and create knowledge. Students are active participants in the construction process of their own knowledge (Thomas, 2000). Successful learners are active, goal-directed, self-regulated, and assume responsibility for contributing to their learning where their learning is influenced by the extent to which they are empowered to embrace the learning process. In this vein, teachers in the learner-centered context must be capable and qualified to teach. Several reports have revealed that having a skilled and knowledgeable teacher is a strong determinant of student learning (Darling-Hammond, 2000). In Rosenhotz's (1989) study concerning school as a workplace, teachers who felt supported through teacher networks, who had cooperation among colleagues, and who had expanded professional roles increased their effectiveness for meeting the needs of students. A body of wisdom about teaching that could be widely shared resulted when teachers had opportunities for collaborative inquiry and began to experiment with new leadership roles (Bryk, Sebring, Kerbow, Rollow, & Easton, 1998).

Throughout your pre-K through grade12 school experience, you complete a series of battery tests, high stakes tests, aptitude tests, summative assessments, and formative assessments. Please ask your school administrators if you could be evaluated on your learning style (Learning Style Inventory) and intellectual ability (Multiple Intelligences). If this is done and thoroughly understood at an early age it could assist and leverage you with the process of learning. I learned and developed my teaching pedagogy in graduate school. Through my pedagogy I was able to discern the type of learners I had in my classes as a classroom teacher and in my buildings as a principal. It would be an advantage for you to understand your "learning pedagogy" at an early age. You would be able to build intellectual capital, bringing increased value to a your self worth. The learner-centered approach, as we know it today, can significantly increase teaching and learning efficiency, because you would be able to self-regulate once introduced to new concepts and new material in your respective classes/subjects.

...thus our students are underserved as much as they are underperforming
– Glenn E. Singleton, Pacific Educational Group, (2003)

Table 3: The Learner-Centered Psychological Principles[1]

Cognitive and Metacognitive Factors

1. *Nature of the learning process.* The learning of complex subject matter is most effective when it is an intentional process of constructing meaning from information and experience.
2. *Goals of the learning process.* The successful learner, over time and with support and instructional guidance, can create meaningful, coherent representations of knowledge.
3. *Construction of knowledge.* The successful learner can link new information with existing information in meaningful ways.
4. *Strategic thinking.* The successful learner can create and use a repertoire of thinking and reasoning strategies to achieve complex learning.
5. *Thinking about thinking.* Higher order strategies for selecting and monitoring mental operations facilitate creative and critical thinking.
6. *Context of learning.* Learning is influenced by environmental factors, including culture, technology, and instructional practices.

Motivational and Affective Factors

7. *Motivational and emotional influences on learning.* What and how much is learned is influenced by the learner's motivation. Motivation to learn, in turn, is influenced by the individual's emotional states, beliefs, interests and goals, and habits of thinking.
8. *Intrinsic motivation to learn.* The learner's creativity, higher order thinking, and natural curiosity all contribute to motivation to learn. Intrinsic motivation is stimulated by tasks the learner perceives to be of optimal novelty and difficulty, relevant to personal interests, and providing for personal choice and control.
9. *Effects of motivation on effort.* Acquisition of complex knowledge and skills requires extended learner effort and guided practice. Without learners' motivation to learn, the willingness to exert this effort is unlikely without coercion.

Developmental and Social Factors

10. *Developmental influences on learning.* As individuals develop, there are different opportunities and constraints for learning. Learning is most effective when differential development within and across physical, intellectual, emotional, and social domains is taken into account.
11. *Social influences on learning.* Learning is influenced by social interactions, interpersonal relations, and communication with others.

Individual Differences

12. *Individual differences in learning.* Learners have different strategies, approaches, and capabilities for learning that are a function of prior experience and heredity.
13. *Learning and diversity.* Learning is most effective when differences in learners' linguistic, cultural, and social backgrounds are taken into account.
14. *Standards and assessment.* Setting appropriately high and challenging standards and assessing the learner as well as learning progress — including diagnostic, progress, and outcome assessment — are integral parts of the learning process.

[1]Taken from *Learner-Centered Psychological Principles: A Framework for School Design and Reform.* American Psychological Association Board of Educational Affairs, December 1995. Also cited by V. G. Thomas. *Learner-Centered Alternatives to Social Promotion and Retention: A Talent Development Approach.* Journal of Negro Education, Vol. 69, No. 4 (Fall 2000).

If we are to help students or individuals who are interested in learning and reaching mastery level in their educational endeavors, we must adhere to the different ways that individuals learn, but moreover, cater to their strengths to prepare them to be confident and competitive in the global community. Tables 4A and 4B on Multiple Intelligence and Learning Style are listed as requirements for students to actively engage and understand how he/she learns. The teachers and mentors should know the student's learning profile as well. This should be a prerequisite to the teaching and learning process for any student or individual interested in succeeding in life.

Table 4A: Multiple Intelligences
Howard Gardner's Multiple Intelligences
(7 Different Ways To Demonstrate Intellectual Ability and Learning Style Inventory 1983)

1. Visual/Spatial Intelligence
ability to perceive the visual. These learners tend to think in pictures and need to create vivid mental images to retain information. They enjoy looking at maps, charts, pictures, videos, and movies.
Skill set:
puzzle-building, reading, writing, understanding charts and graphs, a good sense of direction, sketching, painting, creating visual metaphors and analogies (perhaps through the visual arts), manipulating images, constructing, fixing, designing practical objects, interpreting visual images
Possible Career/Pathways:
navigators, sculptors, visual artists, inventors, architects, interior designers, mechanics, engineers

2. Verbal/Linguistic Intelligence
ability to use words and language. These learners have highly developed auditory skills and are generally elegant speakers. They think in words rather than pictures.
Skill Set:
listening, speaking, writing, storytelling, explaining, teaching, using humor, understanding the syntax and meaning of words, remembering information, convincing someone of their point of view, analyzing language usage
Possible Career/Pathways:
poet, journalist, writer, teacher, lawyer, politician, translator

3. Logical/Mathematical Intelligence
ability to use reason, logic and numbers. These learners think conceptually in logical and numerical patterns making connections between pieces of information. Always curious about the world around them, these learners ask lots of questions and like to do experiments.
Skill Set:
problem solving, classifying and categorizing information, working with abstract concepts to figure out the relationship of each to the other, handling long chains of reason to make local progressions, doing controlled experiments, questioning and wondering about natural events, performing complex mathematical calculations, working with geometric shapes
Possible Career/Pathways:
Scientists, engineers, computer programmers, researchers, accountants, mathematicians

4. Bodily/ Kinesthetic Intelligence

ability to control body movements and handle objects skillfully. These learners express themselves through movement. They have a good sense of balance and eye-hand co-ordination. (e.g. ball play, balancing beams). Through interacting with the space around them, they are able to remember and process information.

Skill Set:

dancing, physical co-ordination, sports, hands on experimentation, using body language, crafts, acting, miming, using their hands to create or build, expressing emotions through the body

Possible Career/Pathways:

Athletics, physical education teachers, dancers, actors, firefighters

---

5. Musical/Rhythmic Intelligence

ability to produce and appreciate music. These musically inclined learners think in sounds, rhythms and patterns. They immediately respond to music either appreciating or criticizing what they hear. Many of these learners are extremely sensitive to environmental sounds (e.g. crickets, bells, dripping taps).

Skill Set:

singing, whistling, playing musical instruments, recognizing tonal patterns, composing music, remembering melodies, understanding the structure and rhythm of music

Possible Career/Pathways:

musician, disc jockey, singer, composer

---

6. Interpersonal Intelligence

ability to relate and understand others. These learners try to see things from other people's point of view in order to understand how they think and feel. They often have an uncanny ability to sense feelings, intentions and motivations. They are great organizers, although they sometimes resort to manipulation. Generally they try to maintain peace in group settings and encourage co-operation. They use both verbal (e.g. speaking) and non-verbal language (e.g. eye contact, body language) to open communication channels with others.

Skill Set:

seeing things from other perspectives (dual-perspective), listening, using empathy, understanding other people's moods and feelings, counseling, cooperating with groups, noticing people's moods, motivations and intentions, communicating both verbally and non-verbally, building trust, peaceful conflict resolution, establishing positive relations with other people.

Possible Career/Pathways:

Counselor, salesperson, politician, business person

---

7. Intrapersonal Intelligence

ability to self-reflect and be aware of one's inner state of being. These learners try to understand their inner feelings, dreams, relationships with others, and strengths and weaknesses.

Skill Set:

Recognizing their own strengths and weaknesses, reflecting and analyzing themselves, awareness of their inner feelings, desires and dreams, evaluating their thinking patterns, reasoning with themselves, understanding their role in relationship to others

Possible Career/Pathways:

Researchers, theorists, philosophers

Table 4B: Learning Style Inventory
(4 Types of Learners)

1. Visual Learners learn best by visually seeing and constructing pictures and images.
Visual Learner Profile
Performs better on written tests; mentally stores pictures and images in their brains; remembers faces rather than names
Visual Learner Behaviors
Takes good notes and organizes them; color codes and organizes material; draws mental pictures as references

2. Auditory Learners learn best by listening or as active participant in open-ended discussions
Auditory Learner Profile
Performs better on oral tests; recalls things they hear can verbally; repeat a script word-for-word
Auditory Learner Behaviors
Tape records information that is important to them; listens to audio recordings repeatedly; reads aloud consistently

3. Kinesthetic Learners learn best by acting out or role playing scenarios in which they are constantly in motion.
Kinesthetic Learner Profile
Performs better on tests requiring physical role play and active participation; can act out a script, story, or concept
Kinesthetic Learner Behaviors
Creates stories to recall facts; role plays scenarios to recall facts; puts poetry in motion

4. Universal Learners
Learn best when they combine the visual, auditory, and kinesthetic elements together
Universal Learner Profile
Performs well on multiple types of tests
Universal Learner Behaviors
Code switches their learning style to one that is best suited for any given situation

NO EXCUSES!

Excuses are tools of the incompetent. They build monuments of nothing. Those who specialize in them seldom accomplish anything.

In this country, education has been said to be the great equalizer when it comes life, liberty, and the pursuit of happiness. I challenge the reader to go a little bit deeper to discover the internal resources needed to experience life, liberty, and happiness. Do not worry about the global comparisons in education. Once you thoroughly understand how you learn, it is expected that you will become the great student or professional that you always aspired to become.

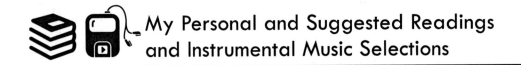 My Personal and Suggested Readings
and Instrumental Music Selections

READ

Delpit, Lisa. (1995). Other People's Children: *Cultural Conflict in the Classroom.* New York: The New Press.

DuBois, William Edward Burghardt. (1973). *the education of black people.* Amhrest: University of Massachusetts Press.

Gould, Stephen J. (1996). *The Mismeasure of Man.* New York: Norton.

Hale, Janice. (1986 revised). *Black Children: Their Roots, Culture, and Learning Styles.* Baltimore: The Johns Hopkins University Press.

Hale, Janice. (2001). *Learning While Black: Creating Educational Excellence for African American Children.* Baltimore: The Johns Hopkins University Press.

Jencks, C. and Phillips, M. (1998). *The Black White Test Gap.* Washington, DC: Brookings Institute Press.

Obiakor, Festus E. and Ford, Bridgie A. (2002). *Creating Successful Learning Environments for African American Learners with Exceptionalities.* Thousand Oaks: Corwin Press.

Perry, Theresa; Steele, Claude; Hilliard, Asa III (2003). *Young Gifted and Black: Promoting High Achievement among African American Students.* Boston: Beacon Press.

Wilson, Amos N. *Awakening the Natural Genius of Black Children (2nd Ed).* New York: Afrikan World Infosystems, 1992

Woodson, C. G. (1933). *The Mis-Education of the Negro.* (10th edition 1998). Trenton: AfricaWorld Press Inc.

Zhao, Y. (2009). *Catching Up or Leading the Way: American Education in the Age of Globalization.* Alexandria: ASCD Publications.

LISTEN

Andre' 3000; *The Art of Storytelling Part 4*

Nas; *Nothing Last Forever*

Outkast; *Liberation*

Chapter 8 Action Item
How would you describe your Learning Style?

Provide a detailed summary explanation of your learning style. This summary should represent a detailed explanation on how you learn, your understanding of how well you learn, and your understanding of when you know that you reached mastery level in all areas of learning educational material.

_____
_____
_____
_____
_____
_____
_____
_____
_____
_____
_____
_____
_____
_____
_____
_____
_____
_____
_____
_____
_____
_____
_____
_____
_____
_____
_____
_____
_____
_____
_____
_____
_____

CHAPTER 9

CONSTRUCT GOOD MORAL CHARACTER AND PREPARE FOR A SUCCESSFUL FUTURE

Objectives

At the completion of this chapter
you will be able to:

Understand the significance of
delaying gratification

Understand the six steps to the
good moral character matrix

Create specific
and relevant SMART goals

Understand the five Ps that lead to success

Understand and effectively implement the
successful future matrix

Perspective

Your integrity is all that you have when it comes to your character. You may be judged by your values, beliefs, and principles. As long as you respect yourself, others will respect you. They may not like you, but they will respect you for your personal stance. Remain humble and grateful for all of your blessings. You must learn the very important construct of delayed gratification! Delayed gratification is a person's ability to wait for something he or she would like. It means waiting to obtain something that is most desired without acting on impulse. This is a trait that individuals with good character exercise frequently. People with good character do not procrastinate and do not depend on their gifts and talents; they simply work hard every day to make improvements. Talent means nothing without practice. People with good moral character develop a thorough understanding of their self-worth. They develop self-respect and do not confuse it with their confidence. They build a strong intellectual and educational foundation in which they continue to aspire for higher achievements. Simply put, these are the things you must do! You must discipline yourself in preparation for a productive life as an adult. You must work! Work! Work! Understand that you are not where you want to be in life, and you should take full advantage of your support systems, i.e., positive peers, family, mentors, teachers, community members, and school personnel.

The best advice I can give you is to learn from your mistakes and make provisions, so that you do not repeat the mistakes. Ask people for constructive criticisms of your actions. Your actions should be guided by your values, standards, and self-respect. Beware of the blind obsessions and blind allegiances to the material delusions that will prevent you from experiencing true ways of living. Keep your eyes open and seek the visual truth of determination and courage which are essential to developing and sustaining good moral character. Reveal your unshakable conviction for a life of good moral character by making improvements every day (Table 5).

Obedience to high principles may require separation from certain people,
even your closest relatives, including your parents, sisters, and brothers –
if they are allied with a destructive principle, group, or way of life.
– Mordecai Wyatt Johnson, first African American President at Howard University

Table 5: Good Moral Character Matrix

Monitor your Appearance

As kids, we followed a certain model when we played football (90% mental – 10% physical) "look good, feel good, play well." We always felt that we played our best when we looked our best. Guys would spat their shoes and wear their uniforms a certain way as a mental edge. Modern day society looks at this behavior as "hotdog behavior or flossing." Psychologically it was our way of mentally playing the game and having something to feel good about internally and externally.

Intrinsic: The Game is won by those who work hardest in preparation during the off season and during the week prior to the game and with love for the game

Extrinsic: Play the way you feel, with excitement, and enthusiasm

Critical Note

Dress neat, groom yourself, and no one should have to tell you to pull your pants up

---

Create a list of sustainable behaviors for yourself

It is your duty to develop a personal handy reference guide on behaviors that speak to your character. Here is a list of characteristics: be fair, be honest with yourself and others, be noble, study often, persevere, be trustworthy, take care of your body, read everything, have nerve, develop your talents, show compassion, extend your services to others, volunteer, respect your teachers and mentors, give 100%, do things in moderation, and reflect on your behaviors.

Support other people's causes and endeavors

It is important that you support other people with their aspirations. Life is full of different people with different experiences and different causes. Support your friends in all that they do. Give your time to other people and other causes that support humanity. Do not think that everybody knows how you feel and what you stand for. Get out there and demonstrate your character through your actions.

Enjoy and reflect on your childhood and teenage years

Like football in which there are 3 phases to the game, i.e., offense, defense, and kicking game, there are also three phases of life—childhood, young adult, and senior living. You are not guaranteed to reach each phase, but you must be prepared to do well at each phase. It is your childhood and teenage years in which you set the precedent for living a productive life. Understand that this is the time that your brain expands and absorbs knowledge at optimum levels. It is imperative that you learn and manifest all that you can at this phase.

Critical Note

There many ill-prepared young people who are struggling in society today. Moreover, research indicates that 1 out of every 2 African American males between the ages 15-24 will be deceased, incarcerated, or unemployed. (College Board, 2011)

Quality time with family members and friends

While growing up, my Aunt Claudia Robinson used to tell me, "Our family is our greatest asset." Having a close family connection is very important. Based on several aspects in society today, we are living in difficult times, and it is critical that you draw strength from your family. More importantly, your family is looking to you for strength! Repeatedly tell your loved ones that you love them. Your family members are the individuals who will tell you the truth, and you must be grateful for that truth and make any adjustments to improve upon your character.

Seek criticism from family and friends

It is good to be proactive rather than reactive. Your family and friends will keep you grounded and on the right track toward your goals. More importantly, be transparent and adhere to suggested changes and recommendations. Make certain that you thank people when they praise you on your efforts of demonstrating good moral character. **You must understand the distinction between family members and family members who are also your friends.**

The tragedy of life is not failing to reach your goal. The tragedy of life is not having a goal to reach. It is not a disaster if you are unable to capture your ideal, but it is a disaster to have no ideal to capture.
It is not a disgrace not to reach the stars, but it is a disgrace to have no stars to reach for.
–Dr. Benjamin E. Mays

Most African American parents want their children to reach higher educational and occupational status than they obtained. High expectations from parents are essential to student achievement. However, reproduction theorists, in contrast, show that schools actually reinforce social inequality while pretending to do the opposite (MacLeod, 1987). Giroux (1983) contends that, "students whose families have a tenuous connection to forms of cultural capital highly valued by the dominant society are at a decided disadvantage." Moreover, Bourdieu (1977) states that "children's academic performance is more strongly related to parents' educational history than to parents' occupational status." Epstein (1994) asserts that strategies intended to develop and direct academic connections between the parent and child are only meaningful when embedded in an understanding of how all the key players in the child's life affect student growth and learning. Coleman's (1988) framework focuses on the degree and quality of social support innate in a young person's interpersonal network. Wynn, Richman, Rubenstein, Little, Britt & Yoken (1987) believe that children and youth from low socio-economic backgrounds, who develop active relationships with institutional representatives across significant social areas, increase their chances for educational success. Relationships with institutional representatives, and the networks that merge these relationships into units, can be understood as social capital (Stanton-Salazar, 1997).

Peer influences on student achievement are critical elements when looking at African American youth. Relationships with peer groups within and outside of school also have a solid and direct impact on student achievement (Coleman & Hoffer, 1987). A pupil's achievement is strongly related to the educational backgrounds and aspirations of the other pupils in the school; this is particularly true of at-risk children (Coleman, 1988). Peer groups can provide incentives to high achievement or distractions and disincentives; they determine whether the associations and casual discussions outside the classroom support or undermine the educational mission of the school and the students. In some schools nearly all students' social relationships beyond the family revolve around the community of youth in the school (Wynn et al., 1987). Adolescent relationships with peers affect their beliefs about the value of school, their own academic competence, their motivation and subsequent academic achievement (Steinberg, 1996). Peer influence accounts for achievement motivation, particularly when a positive relationship is established with a close friend. Parents are thought to be most influential regarding their children's long-term educational plans. However, peers exert more influence on daily behaviors. Students who received both parental and peer academic support were more likely to have academic success (Steinberg, 1996).

Many African American parents place great importance on educational attainment, hard work and good moral values. Luster and McAdoo (1996) noted that African American parents identified educational attainment as the primary strategy for their children to help them succeed in a racially prejudiced society. The parents of high achieving African Americans exhibited optimism and faith in their children's ability to perform well. They frequently communicated with the school, their children's older siblings, and members of the community about academic preparation and progress. On the other hand, parents of low achieving students were overwhelmed by stress, felt they had little control, and exhibited signs of depression. In addition, a spirit of defeat was evidenced in their homes. The home environment varies noticeably among families with similar financial backgrounds, and many children from families of low socioeconomic status do succeed in school when the home environment is supportive (Lee, 1984; Prom-Jackson, Johnson, & Wallace, 1987; Scott-Jones, 1987). These scholars also believe that high achieving African American children from low income, single parent families, had parents who nurtured their children, had high expectations for their children, had good communication with them, had high regard for reading, monitored television programs watched by their children, maintained structured households, and established a system of rewards and punishment for their children. These parents were fully aware of their precarious position in society, but possessed a sense of conviction in their own abilities and a determination to have their children mature into high achieving adults.

I highly recommend that you utilize this simple formula: begin with the end in mind! The prerequisite for success starts with a healthy mind. Find a quiet place where you can think, reflect, and count your blessings. Think about your blessings while you reflect on your challenges. Moreover, think about the opportunities and possibilities of turning your challenges into triumphs. Clearing your head and developing a healthy mind is critical for the mental preparation for a successful future. A successful future starts with setting goals and working hard to reach those goals. Whether you set short-term or long-term goals write down those goals and keep them in a sacred place where you can physically see your goals daily. Use the SMART system when establishing your goals. Ensure that your goals are: Specific, Motivational, Accountable, Responsible, and Touchable (Table 6). Create an action plan which maps out the details leading up to reaching your goals. Set a realistic timeline for you to reach your goals. Consider obstacles and unforeseen issues that may arise and may cause you to adjust your timetable. Chart your progress as you approach the completion of your actions to meet your goals. Involve your parents and your mentor in this process.

Table 6: SMART Goals	
S = SPECIFIC	Can your goal be broken into smaller steps?
M = MOTIVATIONAL	Is it emotionally charged? Do you have the energy to reach your goal?
A = ACCOUNTABILITY	Can your actions toward your goal be tracked and accounted for?
R = RESPONSIBLE	Will it cost you friends? Respect from family? Your integrity?
T = TOUCHABLE	What will you have to hold as a completed result?

Success is to be measured not so much by the position that one has reached in life ... as by the obstacles which he has overcome.
– Booker T. Washington

You **MUST** establish a solid foundation with which to build upon the key elements that lead to a successful future. Remember the five **Ps** as you work towards your future. **P**roper **P**reparation **P**revents **P**oor **P**erformance. Utilize these five **Ps** as a reminder as you assess, chart, and evaluate your progress.

One important key to success is self-confidence.
An important key to self-confidence is preparation.
- Arthur Ashe

The Successful Future Matrix (Table 7) speaks to the key elements that will lead you to reaching and sustaining your goals.

Table 7: Successful Future Matrix

Complete an Ecological Assessment Identify all of the environmental elements that will contribute or interfere with your goals. Utilize your learned skills and prepare for success.	**Be relentless with your work habits** Discipline yourself to stay the course regardless of the challenges. Others will work with you based upon the self-respect you establish by staying motivated and keeping a positive attitude.
Align your resources up with your future plans Be sure to involve everyone who supports you and your goals. It is important that you keep honest people in your inner circle that will remind you of your behaviors and activities that are consistent with your demonstrated character	**Never lose sight of your priorities** Live your life based upon your established principles and values that guide your behaviors. Never doubt what you set out to do and do not think less of what you are doing based upon someone else's standards for living.
Set and monitor your goals daily Create and post your goals in a place where you can see them daily. Make sure your goals are realistic but more importantly make sure your action plan is aligned with to your goals.	**Research and seek advice from those who have reached similar goals** Remember that for what you are attempting to do you can find someone who has already successfully reached these goals. Heed their advice especially when there is no obligation to you.
Mentally prepare for success by developing the right attitude Base your decisions on how you feel about yourself and your future. Believe you can! Believe that you will achieve what you set out to do.	**Reflect on your blessings, challenges, and life experiences** Do not rest on your laurels or previous accomplishments. Do not think that you have to make changes to your plans and goals because of an unforeseen challenge. Stay the course and reflect on your purpose for living your life the way you do.

NO EXCUSES!

Excuses are tools of the incompetent. They build monuments of nothing. Those who specialize in them seldom accomplish anything.

I enjoy helping others. I recall one day in April 2006, when a young man, fresh out of Morehouse College, came to visit my family in Washington, DC. This young man had a lot on his heart at the time. He and I had a man-to-man talk about his future. He expressed with great enthusiasm that he wanted to follow in my foot steps and attend graduate school at Howard University. However, the following day, my wife sat down with him and had a similar conversation, but she was not convinced of his conviction or commitment. She told him candidly that he should consider utilizing his undergraduate degree by taking a year off from school to work. This would afford him the opportunity to seriously consider if graduate school was what he wanted to pursue.

He stuck with his initial decision to pursue a graduate degree at Howard. Fortunately, I was able to assist him by writing letters, presenting him to the committee as a strong candidate, and leading the discussions about him receiving a grad assistant position, which would cover his tuition, room and board, and a provide a monthly stipend. As a result of our efforts, he gained acceptance into Howard with the grad assistant position and its benefits. After one year, he left Howard University. Unfortunately, he did not alert me of his plans. When I called university officials to check his progress, I found out that he dropped out two months prior.

I tell students all the time, "You don't owe me anything, but I owe you everything." The irony of this story is that if had I known that he was not truly committed to this endeavor, I could have helped him with other pursuits and could have helped someone who was better suited to take advantage of the Howard graduate position—someone who might have completed that two-year degree program. I cannot say I am disappointed that he left Howard. Things happen in life that cause people to make tough choices. However, I will say that I am disappointed that he did not take the time to candidly discuss his new decision with me, just as he did initially. The tragedy in this experience is that I was not afforded the opportunity to continue to help this young man.

Weak people cannot be sincere.
–La Rouchefoucauld

My Personal and Suggested Readings and Instrumental Music Selections

READ

Achebe, Chinua. (1959). *Things Fall Apart.* New York: Doubleday

Foster, Chad. (2005). *Financial Literacy For Teens: The Teen's Guide to the Real World of Money.* Conyers: Rising Books.

Franklin, R. M. (1990). *Liberating Visions: Human Fulfillment and Social Justice in African American Thought.* Minneapolis: Fortress Press.

Graham, Steadman. (1998). You Can Make It Happen: A Nine-Step Plan for Success. New York: Fireside

Kiyosaki, R. & Lechter, S. (2004). *Rich Dad Poor Dad for Teens: The Secrets about Money– That You Don't Learn in School!* New York: Time Warner Book Group

Munroe, Myles. (1992). *Releasing Your Potential: Exposing the Hidden You.* Shippensburg: Destiny Image Publishers.

Polite, Vernon C. and Davis, James E. (1999). *African American Males in School and Society: Practices and Policies for Effective Education.* New York: Teachers College.

Stephens, Brooke M. (1999). *Wealth Happens One Day at a Time: 365 Days to a Brighter Future.* New York: HarperCollins Publishers, Inc.

Washington, Joe. (2006). *Breaking the Spirit of Average: 7 Keys to Turn Your Average Into Awesome.* Snellville: Self-published.

LISTEN

AZ; *Give Me Yours*

Common; *Faithful*

J Dilla; *Look of Love Part 1*

Mos Def; *Modern Marvel*

Outkast; *Aquemini*

Raphael Saadiq; *Good Man*

Chapter 9 Action Item
How would you describe character and its relationship to a Successful Future?

Provide a detailed summary explanation of your character and your future projections. This summary should represent a detailed explanation on how you plan to achieve your goals and state how your goals are aligned with your character.

_____
_____
_____
_____
_____
_____
_____
_____
_____
_____
_____
_____
_____
_____
_____
_____
_____
_____
_____
_____
_____
_____
_____
_____
_____
_____
_____
_____
_____
_____
_____
_____
_____
_____
_____

CHAPTER 10

NUMBERS

All progress is precarious,
and thus the solution of one problem brings us
face-to-face with another problem.
– Dr. Martin Luther King, Jr., *Strength to Love* (1963)

Introduction

As a child, my dreams and thoughts about success were immeasurable. I cared about winning, but not at all cost. In an environment characterized by negativity, I always took calculated risks and based my decisions "on the numbers." Winning at all cost in my neighborhood meant severe consequences. It was very common to hear my peers and adults in my neighborhood throwing out numbers about things that were, in my opinion, unworthy of discussion. Phrases such as, he was suspended from school for 10 days; she was expelled from school for 90 days; he was sentenced to 10-25 years in prison; only 10% of the parents attended the academic awards ceremony; 90% of the parents attended the football game; and the list goes on. I wanted to take this time to share with you some of the real numbers that exist in my life.

Furthermore, I want you to take heed and add up some of the positive things that are happing in your life—past, present, and future. This chapter was designed to help you win by understanding the wins and losses you have encountered. I had to look defeat in the face on many levels, but every defeat got me one more step closer to a win. I lost a lot of things in life, but I never lost my integrity, nor do I plan to ever relinquish my integrity to anyone or anything. The best advice I can lend to anyone is that you win in life when you help others succeed. Numbers do not lie, so prepare to face the truth and move on with your journey.

Here are some of the numbers that are relevant to my life, as well as some that may be relevant to yours:

- 0 criminal background hits (no record)
- 1st generation college student and graduate: (BA, M.Ed., Ed. D. Formula: $3°{\uparrow}0 = 3$ degrees above zero)

- 1st Recipient of the Matt Ramser Award. Each spring the Kent State football program presents an award honoring the memory of Matt Ramser, a former scholarship winner who battled cancer for more than two years. The award is given to a member of the football program who best exemplifies the qualities of "courage, dedication, attitude and commitment" that Ramser did in his fight with the disease that claimed his life on January 15, 1992. In addition, the staff has designated the Matt Ramser Award as one that recognizes the greatest improvement in spring drills. After receiving a football scholarship from Kent State in February 1989, Ramser was diagnosed with cancer in May of that same year. (inaugural recipient 1992).

- 1 out of every 2 African American males between the ages 15-24 will be deceased, incarcerated, or unemployed. (College Board, 2011)

- 1 out of every 3 African American males between the ages of 20-29 are under some form of criminal justice control—prison, jail, parole, or probation. (Mauer, 1995).

- 4 founders of Omega Psi Phi Fraternity, Inc. 1911: The Honorable Dr. Ernest E. Just (1883-1941); The Honorable Professor Frank Coleman (1890-1967); The Honorable Dr. Oscar J. Cooper (1888-1972); and The Honorable Bishop Edgar A. Love (1891-1974). *Manhood, Scholarship, Perseverance, and Uplift.*

- 12 Jewels for Living: (1) knowledge, (2) wisdom, (3) understanding, (4) freedom, (5) justice, (6) equality, (7) food, (8) clothing, (9) shelter, (10) love, (11) peace and (12) happiness.

- 24% of ALL students are deemed college ready according to the ACT.

- 48: I was ruled academically ineligible for intercollegiate athletics my freshman year of college due to Prop 48.

- 60% of incoming 2010 freshmen at universities and colleges need remediation.

- 75% of college students need remediation at the community college level.

- 4 out of 5 of remediated students graduate from high school with GPAs above 3.0 (2011 data from the ACT).

- 1989 Graduated from Woodrow Wilson High School (Youngstown, Ohio).

- 1994 Bachelor of Arts (B.A.) Degree, Kent State University (Kent, Ohio).

- 1997 African Americans made up only 13% of the population, but represented half of the 1.2 million state and federal prisons (548,900 precisely); (Allen J. Beck, Bureau of Justice Statistics, *National Prisoner Statistics*).

- 2000 Master's in Education Degree (M.Ed.), Cleveland State University (Cleveland, Ohio).

- 2004 a star is born: Kevin Harris, Jr., December 30. The birth of my son was an event that single-handedly changed my life.

- 2005 Doctorate of Education Degree (Ed. D.), Howard University (Washington, DC).

2011 College Bound Seniors from the State of Georgia SAT Mean Scores by Ethnicity and Total Sub-Group Test Takers

(source: College Board)

In 2011, 23,300 African American students in the state of Georgia took the SAT which represents 32% of all test takers (Table). This was only second to Whites with 37,895 (52%) test participants. African-American students received an average critical reading score of 428, or 57 points below the general population of Georgia test takers and 69 points below all test takers nationally. Math and writing scores reflected similar gaps. There were 3,897 (5%) Asian students who took the SAT and this group posted the highest mean scores in math and writing, 575 and 518 respectively. The critical reading scores for Asian students were second to Whites, lower by only 3 points. Hispanic students' scores also lagged, but not as much as African Americans' scores.

Table 8: 2011 Georgia SAT Test Score Statistics

Critical Reading		Mathematics		Writing	
White	519	Asian, Pacific Islander	575	Asian, Pacific Islander	518
Asian, Pacific Islander	516	White	518	White	504
American Indian	499	American Indian	496	American Indian	478
Other	496	Other	487	Other	477
Puerto Rican	488	Puerto Rican	483	Puerto Rican	472
Hispanic, Latino	482	Hispanic, Latino	484	Hispanic, Latino	470
No Response	469	Mexican or Mexican American	463	No Response	450
Mexican or Mexican American	457	No Response	460	Mexican or Mexican American	442
Black or African American	428	Black or African American	424	Black or African American	417
AVERAGE	**485**	**AVERAGE**	**487**	**AVERAGE**	**473**

SAT Sub-Groups Tested		Pct. %
White	37,895	52%
Black or African American	23,300	32%
Asian, Pacific Islander	3,897	5%
Hispanic, Latino	1,966	3%
Other	1,841	3%
Mexican or Mexican American	1,682	2%
No Response	1,217	2%
Puerto Rican	465	1%
American Indian	247	0%
TOTAL	**72,510**	**100%**

2011 College Bound Seniors from the State of Georgia
ACT Mean Scores by Ethnicity and Total Sub-Group Test Takers
(source: ACT, Inc.)

In 2011, 15,726 African American students in the state of Georgia took the ACT test which was only second to 20,000 Whites. Statewide, 42,929 students were tested (Table 9). African Americans received a 17.5 composite score across English, Math, Reading, and Science which was 3.1 points below the 20.6 average composite score for all of Georgia and 5.3 points below the highest mean score of all sub-groups.

Table 9: 2011 Georgia ACT Test Score Statistics

Race/Ethnicity	English	Mathematics	Reading	Science
Asian	22.6	25.3	22.8	23.1
American Indian	19.1	20.0	19.9	19.8
Black	16.5	17.8	17.5	17.5
Hispanic/Latino	19.1	20.3	20.4	19.9
Island Pacific	18.1	20.4	19.1	19.5
Two+ Races	20.3	20.6	21.3	20.5
No Response	20.7	21.3	21.6	20.8
White	22.7	22.5	23.2	22.3
ALL STUDENTS	20.1	20.7	20.8	20.3

Race/Ethnicity	Composite	ACT Sub-Group Tested
Asian	22.8	1,772
American Indian	19.9	114
Black	17.5	15,726
Hispanic/Latino	20.1	2,555
Island Pacific	19.4	40
Two+ Races	20.8	1,176
No Response	21.2	1,546
White	22.7	20,000
ALL STUDENTS	22.8	42,929

- 56% of all students graduate from high school in the state of Georgia.

- 46% of all African Americans graduate from high school in the state of Georgia.

- $15.5 billion was the cost to the state of Georgia in lost wages due to dropouts from the class of 2008 alone. (source: Alliance for Excellent Education 2009).

A committee takes hours to put into minutes what can be done in seconds.
– Judy Castrina

What Does "College-Ready" Mean?

At a minimum, being college-ready means having the knowledge, skills and behaviors needed to complete the first year of postsecondary study without remediation. College readiness can be achieved by participating in a rigorous comprehensive learning system that focuses on preparing students to successfully complete quality college-level course-work while in high school. This level of preparation is also necessary for students to be considered career-ready. Students who opt to enter the world of work or delay college after high school graduation also need the knowledge, skills and behaviors defined above.

Why Is College Readiness Important?

Competitive, global work environments require more of our students to succeed in college to be prepared to compete. Studies have shown that only about one in five students who enter high school will earn a college degree (Figure 2).

Figure 2: College Readiness by the Numbers

100	70	44	30	21
|	|	|	|	|
For every 100 ninth-graders...	graduate from high school	enter college	return to college for their sophomore year	earn a bachelor's degree within six years

Source: The National Center for Higher Education Management Systems Progress and Completion Data.

In conclusion, after considering all the above statistics, it is clear that we are experiencing a significant decline in academically prepared students! In most countries, prison is where society sends its failures. However, we are contributing to and shaping the prison industry. This is clearly demonstrated by the alarming rates at which our students are dropping out of school.

Twenty years from now you will be more disappointed by the things you didn't do, than by the ones you did do.
– Mark Twain

NO EXCUSES!

Excuses are tools of the incompetent. They build monuments of nothing. Those who specialize in them seldom accomplish anything.

The one thing you have in common with your peers and competitors is time. What you do with your time will be reflected daily. Time waits for no one. After looking at the data mentioned in this chapter, I urge you to build a personal number line for yourself. With this number line you must consider doing things that move you to the right (positive) side of the number line. My theory on numbers is infinity. Therefore, you must take the approach that all things you do must contribute to something positive and without limits. Before you say or do something negative, count to 1 million. Counting to one million is moving to the right on the number line; therefore, forcing you to deal with positive numbers. Positive numbers are a result of positive actions. However, you must look back and connect your past with the present. Your future is based on the likelihood of consistent behaviors and patterns of your lifestyle. Do not look back or return to anything negative, unless you are subtracting something negative from your life. Your past is history, your present is a gift, but your future is a mystery. Go and open doors because you hold the key to your life.

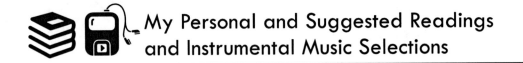

My Personal and Suggested Readings and Instrumental Music Selections

READ

Edelman, Marian W. (1993). *The Measure of Our Success: A Letter to My Children and Yours.* New York: HarperCollins.

Freire, Paulo. (1993). *Pedagogy of the Oppressed.* New York: Continuum.

Hilliard, Asa G. (1991). *Testing African American Students.* Morristown: Aaron Press.

Wright, Richard. (1940). *Eight Men.* New York: HarperCollins.

LISTEN

Amel Larrieux; *Infinite Possibilities*

D'Nell; *Break Reform*

Gaopele; *Salvation*

Nas; *U Gotta Love It*

Souls of Mischief; *From 93 Till Infinity*

Scarface featuring Faith Evans; *Someday*

9th Wonder; *Dream*

9th Wonder; *This Normal Sin*

Chapter 10 Action Item
How would you describe Probability and Statistics?

Provide a detailed summary explanation on how you plan to defy the odds and fulfill your dreams. This summary should represent a detailed explanation of your qualitative plans to overcome some of the depressing quantitative statistics that exist on the local, national, and international levels.

_____

_____

_____

_____

_____

_____

_____

_____

_____

_____

_____

_____

_____

_____

_____

_____

_____

_____

_____

_____

_____

_____

_____

_____

_____

_____

_____

_____

_____

_____

_____

_____

_____

_____

_____

_____

_____

_____

_____

Chapter
11

Heavy Mental

My only true regret, however, is that now that I see the world more clearly than ever, as I believe I do, I don't seem to have the time left to translate my visions into action as I would like.
– Arthur Ashe

Heavy Mental

This chapter is dedicated to all the visual elements that I continue to look to for strength. It is my recommendation that you construct your personal visual canvas where you can draw your successes and also post your visual artifacts that guide you toward your goals. Remember, listening is fundamental, but seeing is believing!

As a child growing up, a black boy with five sisters and no brothers, I was constantly on trial. Twisted in a skein crucible, I wore multiple masks as a method of survival, not conformity. Identity is one of the most important elements for survival. I recall all the names and nicknames I was given, both positive and negative, such as lil black kev, kay-hay, the governor, and the say-hey kid. I learned to wear the masks and play on these nicknames as part of keeping things moving. When we played football I was "the juice" (like O.J. Simpson) on offense, and I was the "say-hey kid" (like Willie Mays) on defense. My longtime friend, Brian Mauzy tagged the nick name Kay-Hay to me in high school. I liked Kay-Hay more than all the other nicknames. It was unique, because it was not far from Willie Mays nickname, and it is a name with a hyphen Kay = Kevin; Hay = Harris; the hyphen represents my life. Like on every head stone, you have a birth date, a hyphen, and a death date. The hyphen represents everything you do between life and death.

Today, I respectfully go by the surname Dr. Kevin Harris. This two letter prefix (Dr.) or a three letter suffix (Ed. D.) is what I earned studying and training under the tutelage of a core group of scholars and practitioners while at Howard University. All societies act on the basis of some sort of shared identity, commonality, ideal, precept, or shared fate. This identity speaks directly to why I chose Howard University to study, train, and earn my terminal degree. A terminal degree is defined as the highest degree in a particular field which ensures the highest level of competence in a particular discipline to certify the person's ability to think independently.

As I think of the language presented in the Howard University School of Education's mission, vision, core values, and strategic focus, **BOLD LEADERSHIP** was the single most important element that stood out to me during my terminal degree search. Remember, people will call you or address you the in context of how you present yourself. Be prepared for the daily challenges of being mentally, psychologically, and intellectually challenged. You are what you believe!

Realizing that all things are not neutral, I still work hard at all things, primarily because I am not naïve and do not believe that I can rest on my laurels or the identity of the entities that I represent. I have made millions of mistakes in my life-time and will make many more. However, when my identity is on trial, please call me as the first, and perhaps the only witness. I am more than happy to tell the truth about all things good or bad.

A setback is a set up for a comeback.
– Willie Jolly

Earned Doctorate at Howard University	
Earned Masters' at Cleveland State	
Earned BA at Kent State	
Earned diploma at Woodrow Wilson High School	

Letter of commendation from US Senator Johnny Isakson (GA)–left *Letter of commendation from Dr. William R. Harvey President, Hampton University–right*	 
Generations of success. The journey continues. *Clockwise from left: Mickey Harris (uncle), Clyde W. Frazier (father), Thommie, Sr. and Minnie Harris (grandparents), Kevin Harris, Sr., Ed.D., Kevin Harris, Jr. (son)*	
Omega Psi Phi Fraternity, Inc. 1911	

Give a man a mask, and he will tell you the truth.
– Oscar Wilde

NO EXCUSES!

Excuses are tools of the incompetent. They build monuments of nothing. Those who specialize in them seldom accomplish anything.

There is no reason why you cannot fulfill your dreams. Dare to dream. Take your mental thoughts and make them visible realities.

 ## My Personal and Suggested Readings and Instrumental Music Selections

READ

Leinwand, G. (1970). *The Consumer: Problems with American Society.* New York: Washington Square Press.

Wright, Richard. (1945). *Black Boy.* New York: HarperCollins.

LISTEN

Branford Marsalis 4tet; *Coltrane's Love Supreme*

Gaopele; *Closer to My Dreams*

J Dilla; *It's Your World*

J Dilla; *Believe*

Talib Kweli; *This is My Life*

9th Wonder; *Warrior Song*

Chapter 11 Action Item
What's on your Mind?

Provide a detailed summary explanation on your mental outlook on life. This summary should represent a detailed explanation of your mental process of turning your dreams into reality. Describe your process of turning your vision into action. What drives you? What motivates you?

_____

_____

_____

_____

_____

_____

_____

_____

_____

_____

_____

_____

_____

_____

_____

_____

_____

_____

_____

_____

_____

_____

_____

_____

_____

_____

_____

_____

_____

_____

_____

_____

_____

_____

_____

_____

_____

_____

_____

_____

The Harris "Choose to Succeed" Framework

As a result of continuous research on theories relating to school reform and as a practitioner of public K-12 education as a student, teacher, assistant principal, principal, and consultant for more than 22 years, I have decided to construct the *Harris Choose to Succeed Framework* and also to construct local, national, and international Core Student Standards for K-12 students.

Systemic reform is the process of pinpointing the elements of a complex system and making strategic choices about the layers of influence on change that may yield a high probability of improving critical outcomes (Banathy, 1996). Using the Harris Choose to Succeed Framework (Figure 3) to approach student reform helps us to understand that the external layers can liberate the internal layer and produce extraordinary results. The external layers must be visible to the student's eyes, ears, mind, and heart. These layers represent the core platform in which the student stands on for strength, guidance, support, and victory. As part of the initiation segment of the Harris Choose to Succeed Framework all people, support personnel, and internal/external elements must be identified. A collaborative success plan must be created with the student's academic achievement and personal development goals at the center of the framework. It is understood that change must be made at multiple levels to see results.

The most significant change in a student's life must start with a change internally. In any change-oriented organization, information is made available at all times. With the Harris Choose to Succeed Framework, the student must ascertain and know all the information about self—good or bad. This will enable the student to adjust to his/her surroundings with dignity. This also helps the student to set realistic goals and objectives. This framework helps students to structure and facilitate change efforts with academic achievement and personal development. This framework also visually represents the varying levels of effort and support that contribute to academic achievement and personal development. Although these elements exist, we will not use race, class, gender, economics, and poverty in particular, as excuses. The four inner layers of the framework are interconnected via self-identity and collaboration. The external layer, in many cases of urban school students, represents the cause and the effect. This is the layer that the Framework was designed to debunk. When student efforts and the support systems are maximized or in sync with one another the result is that a successful student is ready to engage, develop, and live a successful life.

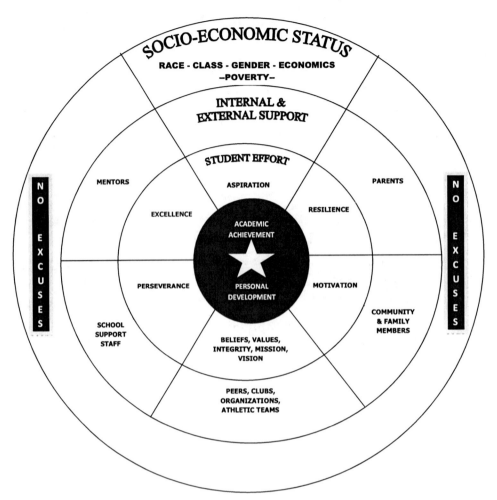

Figure 3 Harris Choose to Succeed Framework

The Student

The Harris Choose to Succeed Framework is conceptualized through a systems approach, rooted in self-actualization as a mechanism to achieve academically and to develop personally. The objective is for each student to find the star within. When you believe that you are a star you will begin to work like a star. Stars expect greatness. Stars expect to reach high academic achievement levels. Stars work hard on their strengths and challenges. Personal development is the primary focal point of the stars. Stars practice on a regular basis with high expectations of making improvements every day. I pose these questions to any person: Are you a star? Do you have the potential to become a star? Do you have the superstar potential? Regardless of your answers, nothing is actualized without a base and the five elements listed in the second layer. No matter what you aspire to become, personal development is the prerequisite of reaching and sustaining your goals and objectives.

The Effort

How learning environments are established and maintained rests on the skills and creativity of the teachers and other practitioners (Darling-Hammond, 2000). However, it is the innate abilities, wherewithal, the *it*, and all other adjectives that describe the student's unexplainable passion and work traits that lead to success. The Choose to Succeed Framework identifies five core elements: *(1) aspiration (2) resilience (3) motivation (4) perseverance and (5) excellence* . These five core elements of student effort are grounded by the student's **base beliefs, values, integrity, mission and vision**. It can be stated that possessing a strong and unwavering base can lead to positive outcomes along your journey.

Furthermore, it should be noted that, if the aforementioned five core elements are well designed and implemented, the student will prosper and experience optimal success. In addition, your supporting cast (parents, mentors, teachers, school support staff, and peers) will favorably push the student to reach higher levels of success. I want to be clear in stating that the overall support for any student is contingent upon his/her internal efforts. For example, when students reach the undergraduate level of continuing their education, it is expected by the professors that the students have been exposed to certain texts and have a maturity level to understand what is expected. Each of the five core elements are important features of the student's achievement and personal development. This layer of the framework deals with the mental stamina needed for students to reach greatness later in life.

After talking with successful people from all walks of life, I will tell you that all of them contribute at least one of the five core features in layer two as a prominent element(s) that contributes to their continued success. Successful people possess a solid base facilitated by internal and external support which represents layer three, the support systems of the framework.

The Support Systems

While the core elements of the framework are most directly associated with student-driven success and accountability, the support systems layer serves as the coverage layer for each student. This layer is equivalent to having life insurance. When a student is supported by his/her *(1) parents; (2) community and family members; (3)peers, club/organization members, athletic teammates; (4) school support staff; and (5)mentors,* the student is able to engage in sustainable and continued improvement efforts to succeed and reach his/her goals. This framework was designed to have students at the center, while at the same time, facilitating their input in the success process. Often, students see the big picture as a traditional authoritative approach. However, this framework was designed for students to solicit and embrace the support needed for them to have a diverse experience. This layer of the framework calls for the student to communicate and articulate all of the elements of his/her internal fabric, as well as the first layer of the framework to his/her support systems. This is the layer where the students establish priceless relationships, gain valuable perspectives on life, and have their goals and efforts evaluated objectively by people they trust.

It is critical that the students acquire key people to work with them toward academic achievement and personal development. This perhaps is one of the biggest challenges that a student may face, due to the fact that people are mobile and they do not stay in one place over long periods of time. Furthermore, it is a way to manage student improvement by a diverse group of people with skills to see the vision and facilitate growth and development for the student.

The Myth

You must believe that your current family income does not necessarily represent your future financial income or your personal outcome. It has been well documented that many children living in poverty have turned out to be successful people. Moreover, when one believes that he/she will succeed in spite of race, class, gender, and economics, they indeed succeed! Regardless of your race, class, gender, or socioeconomic status, you must develop a blueprint for success. This layer of the framework is important because students must embrace who they are and begin to work on improvement, in spite of their living conditions and academic expectations from other people.

There are two types of people in this world: *the haves and the have nots*. The **haves** are characterized by possessing social, cultural, financial, and educational capital. Whereas the **have nots** are characterized by those waiting for something or somebody to hand them something without any investment. Many people who grew up in poverty have developed a framework or a blueprint to succeed in life and have created a mental expectation to become one of the **haves**. It's also important to note that many individuals who experienced success after growing up poor give back to the communities from which they came from.

I stress the fact that many students struggle to find where they are going or find it difficult to establish a destination, because they do not truly understand or perhaps acknowledge where they came from (– Sankofa).

Summary

In spite of some of the best and brightest students coming from urban, diverse communities and backgrounds, the results of African American academic achievement and personal development in the United States remains unsatisfactory on multiple levels. This reality continues to plague this group of students and society as a whole. The narrow impact of much school reform has led me to construct The Harris Choose to Succeed Framework, a more personal approach to academic achievement and personal development. This particular framework examines the student and the interrelationships between its core parts. The Harris Choose to Succeed Framework is essential, because it allows the student to express what is internally and externally important and embrace the support mechanisms needed to achieve the established goals and objectives. The Harris Choose to Succeed Framework provides a platform that allows students to find strength and salvation from within as part of the paradigm shift toward academic achievement and personal development. Students must be able to lead now, if we expect them to scale up and lead in the future. If we examine society in the purest context of sustainability, we must invest in our renewable resources, the students!

Too many of us see education as essentially a preparation for jobs, as a preparation for moving up in social status, and as a means of securing a better lifestyle. And certainly, these are some of its major functions. However, I do not see them as the primary functions of education. I think it is vital that we understand that the major function of education is to help secure the survival of a people.
–Amos Wilson (1992)

The major focus of school reforms over the past two decades has been the changing role of the principal, because the principal is viewed as the key agent for change within the school (Dow & Oakley, 1992; Sergiovanni, 1990). Dow and Oakley (1992) found that school effectiveness literature indicated that principal leadership was "an essential ingredient in creating and maintaining an effective school." Sergiovanni's work indicates that the key to quality schooling is the "amount and kind of leadership that the school principal provides…"

Many scholars maintain that the school systems, as they currently operate, are unprepared to offer the support children desperately need in light of changing family, financial, and community designs (Coleman, 1987; Jones, 1989; Pine & Hilliard, 1990). However, effective schools for poor minority students have historically shared common characteristics, including a strong principal, a climate of high expectations where no child is allowed to fall below prescribed levels, and a strategy for closely monitored scholastic progress (Edmonds, 1979).

African Americans and other minority youth are often forced to achieve traditional developmental tasks within environments where there is constant conflict that creates barriers to their customs, beliefs, and cultural norms (Boykin, 1986). For some high achieving African American students, success is perceived by their peers in a negative way. Kunjufu (1986) found that some high-achieving African Americans become class clowns to conceal their academic abilities. This notion is identified in other students who live dual lives, adopting the norms and values of the majority culture to achieve success in school, while embracing African American cultural norms outside school to attain social acceptance.

African Americans historically have been plagued by low teacher expectations, inequitable educational opportunities, and school underachievement, often leading to their disproportionate placements in special education programs for children with disabilities (Losen & Orfield, 2002). One of our greatest challenges is to successfully educate African American children and the school-family community-at-large.

From the literature on school effectiveness (Comer, 1986; Edmonds, 1979) a clear picture emerges of those characteristics of the family, school, and community environments that may alter or even reverse expected negative outcomes and enable individuals to circumvent life stressors and manifest resilience. Caring relationships, positive and high expectations, and opportunities for meaningful participation are related factors that help students succeed. Several educational reformers believe that when schools ignore these basic needs for both students and teachers, the schools become alienating places (Sarason, 1982).

The School Development Program (SDP), otherwise known as the Comer Process, puts children at the center of the educational process. It calls on significant adults in children's lives at home, in school, and the community to work together to support and nurture every child's total development, so each can reach his or her full potential. At the core of the SDP is a focus on holistic child development along six pathways – physical, speech and language, moral, social, psychological, and academic. Its basic premise is that all children have the potential to succeed in school and in life, and that the realization of this potential depends on how well educators, families, and communities work together to create environments that support child development. The creation of a supportive school climate that nurtures and sustains good psychosocial development and high levels of academic performance is of central importance to the SDP (Anson, Cook, Grady, Haynes, & Comer, 1991).

Core Student Standards

It is with great enthusiasm that I introduce the **Core Student Standards** on personal development that contribute to academic achievement and success in life as the essential method for student reform. I am sincere about my approach to get students to think seriously about themselves in an effort to make significant contributions to society. My approach is geared toward fixing and sustaining a system of self. Many of our students lack social skills and critical thinking skills in particular; they have much difficulty with complex challenges that require thinking and processing. Not to mention, all of our students **possess** the innate ability to function at optimum levels, but have yet to consistently engage the instructors, coaches, teachers, mentors, and leaders who are interested in their teaching and learning process for survival and success.

MENTORSHIP

(left) Fred Sands IV, 2012 Valedictorian, Carver SOTA High School, Atlanta, Georgia; accepted to Howard University. (middle) MENTOR: Kevin Harris, Sr., Ed.D., 2005 Howard University graduate, education administration, leadership and policy major. (right) Ricky Lipsey, 2011 Valedictorian, Therrell STEMS High School, Atlanta, Georgia; successfully completed first year at Howard University with studies in business marketing, (actuarial sciences major).

CORE STUDENT STANDARD #1

The highly motivated and high-achieving student develops and articulates a personal vision, mission, and values which he/she shares with parents, peers, mentors, and school staff.

The highly motivated and high-achieving student has a dual focus—academic achievement and personal development. This student, with the help and support from parents, mentors, and school personnel, understands what needs to be done, and develops a blueprint on how to accomplish established goals and objectives. High expectations and high standards are what guide the student's actions.

Rationale: Students can work more effectively and efficiently when they have input in their own development and when their personal vision, mission, and values are clear and collaboratively agreed upon by parents, mentors, and school staff. Students will achieve academic and personal success when they decide that academic and personal success is what they want for self.

Implementation Strategies: Some of the various strategies students should consider for implementing this standard:

- Solicit a support system that consists of parents, peers, mentors, and key school personnel to help construct a meaningful vision, mission, and values.

- Institute a system of clear measurable indicators that lead to successful academic achievements and personal development.

- Participate in co-curricular activities and programs that enhance social capital and require critical thinking, deductive and inductive reasoning; use all human and technical resources to establish an objective self-accountability system

Student Practices: Current practices that support this standard:

- Take the highest level of course-work throughout your school career including advanced placement courses, honors courses, accelerated courses, gifted courses etc. Taking these courses further prepares the student for post-secondary matriculation into top colleges and universities of choice and quality academic work while on campus.

- Work diligently with your parents, peers, mentors, and school staff to ensure that shared decision-making is the outcome of critical thinking sessions and mentoring sessions.

- Volunteer in the community and lend support to solving problems and challenges that impact the community.

Assignment: Interview a well-respected, top performing CEO and ask if the company's vision, mission, and values are important to the organization. Ask for an explanation of the company's five-year strategic plan.

The highly motivated and high-achieving student develops high expectations and high standards for self.

The highly motivated and high-achieving student expects to meet and exceed personal, local, district, state, national, and international standards academically. The highly motivated and high-achieving student possesses a belief system that he/she can learn at high levels and work at or beyond their potential.

Rationale: Highly motivated and high achieving students believe and demonstrate greatness and show appreciation to others around them. They Do NOT make excuses!

Implementation Strategies: Some of the various strategies students should consider for implementing this standard:

- Recognize your intellectual gifts and work at better utilizing them every day. "Practice makes what? <u>IMPROVEMENT!</u>"

- Be visible throughout your school and community by actively participating in academic-related activities during and after school. Represent yourself and your school in local, state, national, and international workshops and competitions.

- Make sure that you meet and exceed the required advanced placement, international baccalaureate, honors, and accelerated course requirements and benchmarks throughout your K-12 school career.

- Develop specific plans to gain college credits while in high school. In addition, develop specific plans to work as an intern or an apprentice under a trusted and well-vetted mentor/firm associated with your career aspirations.

Student Practices: Current practices that support this standard:

- Sign-up and take the PSAT and the PLAN (Pre-ACT) as early as 7th grade and continue to study and train in those areas throughout middle and high school. Use the data to thoroughly prepare for the National Merit Scholarship Qualifying Program.

- Work with your English teacher or a writing specialist to improve your writing and critical thinking skills. Write multiple drafts of personal statements for college entrance and scholarship opportunities. In addition, work with a math and science specialist to prepare to exceed standards on the Trends in International Mathematics and Science Study (TIMMS) assessments.

- Apply for summer enrichment programs at major colleges/universities such as Claflin, Cleveland State, Columbia, Duke, Emory, Georgetown, Georgia Tech, Hampton, Harvard, Howard, Johns Hopkins Medical, Kent State, Meharry Medical, Morehouse Medical, North Carolina, Ohio State, Southern California, South Carolina State, Spelman, Stanford, Tuskegee, Virginia State, University of Georgia and Youngstown State.

The highly motivated and high-achieving student develops a dedicated spirit, gaining meaningful skills through personal development and the creation of a positive personal brand.

The highly motivated and high-achieving student commits to his/her own personal development while working collaboratively with mentors and coaches to develop a personal brand. The highly motivated and high-achieving student recognizes the importance of renewal and works to sustain the characteristics associated with motivation, success, ingenuity, intelligence, and nobility.

Rationale: Highly motivated and high-achieving students know the importance of sacrifice and hard work to improve their skill sets and character traits.

Implementation Strategies: Some of the various strategies students should consider for implementing this standard.

- Seek mentors and mentorship programs that are aligned with one's beliefs. Seek opportunities for multiple types of coaching and mentoring.

- Attend peer assistance and peer review trainings to enhance one's knowledge and develop and refine your social, leadership, and life skills.

- Take at least two trade/career technical classes that lead to industry certification to ensure value to one's future education, business, and personal endeavors.

- Establish a non-profit or LLC and take advantage of the benefits of business ownership.

- Work with mentors and coaches to construct a personal growth plan.

Student Practices: Current practices that exist to support this standard:

- To date, students are part of mentoring programs all across the world. Many students attend the post-secondary collegiate programs for middle/high school students during the summers.

- Many mentoring programs across the nation work in conjunction with colleges and universities to support student enrollment in pre-college programs.

- The Congressional Black Caucus, The National Association of Secondary School Principals, and the National Honor Society offer programs that promote the academic and social development of its candidates and participants.

Assignment: Interview a high school or college admissions counselor and ask what do ordinary students do to reach extraordinary levels of success.

CORE STUDENT STANDARD #4

The highly motivated and high-achieving student accepts responsibility and accountability for personal outcomes and will work to improve outcomes and results that are unsatisfactory to their personal expectations and standards.

The highly motivated and high-achieving student understands his/her role in becoming successful by way of an unwavering commitment to excellence. The highly motivated and high-achieving student solicits the support system of individuals who share the responsibility of creating such a platform and provide support every step of the way. The highly motivated and high-achieving student appropriately utilizes available human and academic resources to work toward achieving goals and objectives. In addition, the highly motivated and high-achieving student assesses personal weaknesses and makes adjustments toward improvements daily.

Rationale: "The gem cannot be polished without friction." Anything worth having requires hard work over a period of time. You must go through something in order to become something!

Implementation Strategies: Some of the various strategies students should consider for implementing this standard:

- Engage your parents, mentors, and school staff in your current and future endeavors.

- Assess your present standings (academics, personal, social engagements) to set clear and realistic goals toward personal improvement.

- Assess and evaluate the results of your 4.5- to 6-week Student Reform Assessment Benchmark Evaluation Forms* and devise a strategy for personal development.

- Monitor progress toward your short-term and long-term goals by gathering and reviewing evidence of gains and setbacks with action plans to improve in the areas which need improvement.

Student Practices:

- Work with your parents for a thorough understanding of what is expected of you at home, school, and in the community. Furthermore, make sure you know what your parents are holding you accountable for in terms of your actions, behaviors, and outcomes.

- Work with your school staff, mentors, and mentoring program staff to examine the current accountability systems that are in place.

Assignment: Interview your mentor and ask how accepting responsibility and accountability has led to his/her successes.

*Covered later in this book.

CORE STUDENT STANDARD #5

The highly motivated and high-achieving student values ethics and personal integrity.

The highly motivated and high-achieving student demonstrates ethics and personal integrity with the highest regard to humanity. The highly motivated and high-achieving student demonstrates and models acceptable moral and ethical standards in all interactions and possesses a willingness to respect and honor the rights of all other people's, race, class, culture, ethnicity, origin, gender, and socioeconomics. The highly motivated and high-achieving student demonstrates nondiscriminatory and inclusive ethics and integrity practices.

Rationale: Our nation is experiencing an ethics crisis!

Implementation Strategies: Some of the various strategies students should consider for implementing this standard:

- Ensure that you are exposed to a rich array of viewpoints, perspectives, and experiences that force the student to think critically and which add to worldly discussion and dialogue.

- Engage in substantive, ongoing development and opportunities toward shaping, molding, and instilling ethics and integrity within the student.

- Develop an action plan where diversity is reflected in or among group dynamics and personal development trainings. Commit to a no-harm principle while treating others with humanity.

Students Practices:

- Model moral and ethical behaviors. Promote democracy through your actions.

- Honor commitments with fulfillment when mutually agreed upon by all parties.

- Accept objective awards, recognition, and honors over subjective awards, recognition, and honors.

- Obey parents' rules, student codes of conduct, local, state, and national laws, rules, policies and procedures.

- Present the well-being of self through the fundamental value of ethics and integrity of all decision making and personal actions

Assignment: Interview a respected superintendent, teacher, CEO or principal and ask how they maintain their integrity and remain ethical during critical situations. Ask them to elaborate on their personal challenges and organizational challenges.

The highly motivated and high-achieving student makes connections with post-secondary learning and career options via K-12 vertical articulation alignment for success.

The highly motivated and high-achieving student actively participates in the seamless continuation of academic programs and services that lead to mastery level outcomes in preparation for post-secondary options.

Rationale: Mastery learning is an outcome of early introduction and continuous opportunities to learn new things.

Implementation Strategies: Some of the various strategies students should consider for implementing this standard:

- Begin with the end in mind; build your K-12 school course schedule starting with college career major/minor working backward to your current grade.

- Explore community and business resources that can provide real-world work experiences, job shadowing, high quality apprenticeships, service learning, internships, scholarships and other career development activities and opportunities.

- Learn and master at least two vocational trades to add to and enhance your academic and personal profile.

- Visit your school counselor/advisor on a regular basis to ensure compliance in your career pathway and a successful transition to adult life.

Student Practices:

- Participate in dual and joint enrollment programs that are offered to high school students with specific requirements. Seek graduation with three or more advanced placement courses on your transcript.

- Check out the multiple diploma choices that are being offered to students: college prep, honors, technical, vocational; school-to-work programs (work-based learning) or JROTC research oriented (clinical and practitioner) programs. Also investigate extra-curricular programs with academic accountability standards.

Assignment: Analyze your transcript to ensure your courses are aligned with your (NCAA Clearinghouse) post-secondary career aspirations.

Suggested Reading
Sarason, S. B. (1995). *School Change: The Personal Development of a Point of View.* New York: Teachers College Press.

Conclusion

The current state of education, for African Americans in particular, is complex and represents a myriad of challenges. It is my assertion that the most precious resource, **the student,** has been ignored. In turn, the student has become the critical problem. We turned our attention to reform models that speak to facilities, the physical school building, per pupil expenditures, teaching and learning models, teacher assessment and accountability evaluations, pay-for-performance programs and preparation programs for educators; however, we ignored the students by way of lowering our expectations for the students. We found methods to cater to their deficiencies and not their strengths. We condoned high failure rates and high dropout rates. We continue to find ways to alienate the students and the parents from active participation in the total school program. In the context of school, many of our students have developed a disdain for themselves and for their parents, teachers, administrators, and school board members. They have insulated themselves with a nihilistic approach to society. We have failed.

However, there is an expectation that if we build upon strengths and address the students in the affirmative with respect to the student reform approach and with the appropriate installation of the Core Student Standards, the students will rise! We will rise in totality for public education. "We cannot fix our nation's educational problems until we fix our individual student problems." This approach is grounded in the Harris Choose to Succeed Framework, where the time invested is at the foundation stage. Personal development is also emphasized where we instill a belief system in each student and teach the student about the core principles of aspiration, resilience, motivation, perseverance, and excellence as prerequisites for academic achievement, personal development, and success throughout life.

I believe that this approach will lead African American students to higher academic achievement and personal development levels. I also believe it will foster the achievement and development of all diverse student groups, in particular the students with special needs. Grounded in theoretical and practical research and applications, I contend that student assets are the driving force to addressing student deficiencies. We must approach the transformation process by co-constructing and imposing the student's beliefs, values, integrity, mission, and vision as a way of life. This approach, which is basic to the ethos of African American people, will underscore the historical continuity of education in America for African Americans. We will teach the students about the past and the successful outcomes realized in the face of unparalleled adversity.

The underpinning of the Harris Choose to Succeed Framework is a focus on developing leaders, innovators, discoverers, creators, and liberators. Our students will become the architects of change and the engineers of academic achievement and personal development. We will foster the discovery and creativity in each student. It is my belief that each student must discover:

1. His/herself and the societal factors that influence their behavior

2. His/her creative potential and the cognitive processes which influence intellectual development; and

3. His/her cultural autonomy and the correct response to its essential demands

I have established a new reform model which speaks directly to the students by way of achievement and development and is constructed with specific guidelines, beliefs, values, integrity, mission, vision, thoughts, and images. However, successful implementation of the Harris Choose to Succeed Framework depends on the aspiration, resilience, motivation, perseverance, and excellence (self-actualization and a commitment) from the students. The students need to be well-prepared for the journey. The journey will be heavily influenced by developing the student's personal profile. With the right support and well-thought out, well-conceived, and sustainable plans, the student can approach school and life with confidence, applicable skill sets, and a plethora of resources and support personnel available. It is my position that students should have input in their own development. Therefore, it is important to collect as much qualitative data as possible to construct meaningful and sustainable plans that address the dreadful quantitative data that currently exist.

The chapters in this publication highlight the focused attention our students desperately need. We will not and cannot wait for another reform model that does not focus directly on students. Academic achievement and personal development is not only momentous for African American students in poor urban schools, but also for the economic well-being of the entire global community. My aspirations for academic achievement and personal development remain the fundamental necessity for student success in life. The students must know and understand their own unique story, good or bad, to make universal change toward a discovered purpose. The application of the Harris Choose to Succeed Framework and the Core Student Standards opens the door to self actualization for individuals to discover and sustain greatness.

Dismal statistics presented with little social or historical context have resulted in educational policies and practices that perpetually use a deficit model for black males. The deficit model focuses on problems instead of evaluating strengths.
Whitney Young High School in Chicago, Illinois (predominantly black high school that earned recognition as one of the top schools in the country by U.S. News and World Report) and Davidson Magnet School in Augusta, Georgia are prominent examples of schools that defy existing educational gaps. Likewise, every black community, regardless of economic resources contains shining examples of young men who achieve in school, regardless of immeasurable social disadvantages.
–Ivory Toldson, PhD (2010)

Declarative Pledge to My Teacher

I care too much about you
to act up in your classroom.
Therefore, there is no way
I will disrupt class or interfere
with the teaching and learning process.

There is no way I will allow you to
stop teaching me and my classmates.

There is no way I will interfere
with your enthusiasm to impart
knowledge to me and my classmates.

There is no way I am going to miss
this golden opportunity to learn
from a highly competent
and dedicated scholar.

Ecological Assessment Process

Student Reform
Continuous Self Assessment

Rating Scale: 5 = Excellent   4 = Good   3 = Fair   2 = Poor   1 = Unacceptable

___ **Education** – A clear commitment and focus to the continuous acquisition of new knowledge in order to function as an effective scholar and communicator. **Comments:** _____
_____
_____

___ **Analytic Ability** – The potential to analyze problem situations in depth; make decisions in a methodical, systematic manner; anticipate opposition/ramifications and propose alternative plans of actions, generate realistic solutions to problems, and discern facts without biases or prejudices. **Comments:** _____ _____
_____
_____

___ **Leadership Abilities** – The potential to provide leadership in a school, business, judicial, social, political, or athletic setting that is results oriented; able to provide executive level leadership to peers, parents, school staff and mentors in implementing and expanding opportunities for stakeholder involvement; able to implement a broad range of student oriented programs. The potential to work with and meet the needs of culturally diverse settings. **Comments:** _____
_____

___ **Management and Personal Development** – The potential to plan for short and long term goals; to be well organized. The potential to negotiate clear, fair, and challenging goals with self. The ability to mobilize peers and stakeholders; able to create consensus among peers; able to create a climate/culture of harmony. **Comments:** _____
_____

___ **Intellectual and Social Capital** – The ability to deal with a diverse group of people in a broad range of situations and levels. The ability to accurately connect to the feelings and needs of others. The potential to work under pressure and remain calm as well as being able to accept criticism. The potential to juggle several projects and successfully involve others to achieve goals. **Comments:** _____
_____

___ **Climate Match** – The ability to stand on principle when it comes to standing on your beliefs and goals when looking at working with schools and organizations. Ability to convey your expectations and request a list of committed priorities geared at increasing student involvement, achievement, increased learning outcomes, and strengthening of relationships between parents, students, schools, and organizations. **Comments:** _____
_____

___ **Effective Communication Skills** – The ability to think and speak clearly. Ability to code-switch and speak the principle language in any given situation. Able to clarify and organize thoughts; ability to think quickly. Articulate and fluent in use of appropriate vocabulary, grammar, and word usage. The potential for success in maintaining effective communication and working relationships among parents, peers, mentors, and school personnel. **Comments:** _____
_____

Student Reform Assessment
4.5- to 6-Week Benchmark Evaluation Form

Name _____ School/Program_____

5	4	3	2	1
OUTSTANDING	EXCEEDS REQUIREMENTS	MEETS REQUIREMENTS	NEEDS IMPROVEMENT	UNACCEPTABLE
Performance is consistently exceptional in all areas and is recognizable as being superior	Performance is of high quality and is achieved on frequent basis and noted to be above expectations	Competent and dependable level of performance	Performance is deficient in one area. Not meeting the requirements of Student Reform	Unacceptable performance in two areas. Intervention is mandatory; assignment of a mentor is highly recommended

(X) Appropriate Evaluation Below

Judgment
_____ Above average in making decisions
_____ Average in making decisions
_____ Below average in making decisions

Attitude/Application to Work
_____ Very interested and industrious
_____ Above average diligence
_____ Below average in diligence and interest

Dependability
_____ Completely dependable
_____ Above average dependability
_____ Below average dependability

	5	4	3	2	1
Interpersonal Skills Treats self, peers, parents, and school staff with receptiveness, dignity, respect, and professionalism. Demonstrates ability to work successfully in collaboration with parents, peers, school personnel, mentors, and other professionals. Effectively communicates with others. Comments:	5	4	3	2	1
Quality of Work Effective in maintaining and assuring the quality of care and appropriateness of academic work submitted to teachers and school personnel. Comments:	5	4	3	2	1
Personal Development Demonstrates a commitment to attend meetings, tutoring, workshops, and conferences that promote personal growth and development. Seeks expertise in areas identified for improvement. Continuously works at meeting personal goals and objectives. Comments:	5	4	3	2	1

PARENT SURVEY

Student Reform Assessment
4.5- to 6-Week Benchmark Evaluation Form

Please circle **YES** or **NO** in response to each of the following statements.
Provide comments if necessary.

1. The teacher(s) seems to know my child's strengths and needs. Comments:	Yes — No
2. The teacher(s) effectively communicates with me. Comments:	Yes — No
3. The teacher(s) often gives my child rigorous work. Comments:	Yes — No
4. The teacher(s) gives my child the appropriate level of homework. Comments:	Yes — No
5. The school curriculum is meeting the needs of my child. Comments:	Yes — No
6. I rely on my child's report card to let me know how my child is doing in school. Comments:	Yes — No
7. I have met with my child's teacher(s) at least once during this benchmark period. Comments:	Yes — No
8. I feel that my child is treated fairly by his/her peers. Comments:	Yes — No
9. I know my child's goals and objectives for each 4.5 – 6 week Benchmark period. Comments:	Yes — No
10. I believe that my child's teacher(s) has a good rapport with my child. Comments:	Yes — No
11. I communicate with my child on a daily basis about school and his/her goals. Comments:	Yes — No

PERSONAL CODE OF CONDUCT*

UNCONDITIONAL LOVE
If you see all people and all things as an extension of yourself you will treat them as you wish to be treated. Unconditional love requires that one surrender judgment, criticism, and ego.
Note: Love yourself and be ok with that!

TRUTH
Truth is consistent and will not harm anyone. One must accept truth, speak truth, teach truth and seek truth for true spiritual empowerment.
Note: The truth will set you free!

WILLINGNESS
The ability to give up self-centered desire and do what is in accordance with spiritual law.
Note: Not every person is equipped with the internal fabric to sacrifice self for truth and freedom!

RIGHTEOUSNESS
Action based on truth and what is correct for the maintaining of balance and harmony.
Note: Righteousness requires continuous hard work!

RESPONSIBILITY
Being consciously accountable for one's desires and thoughts that manifest into action.
Note: Responsibility is an action word!

DISCIPLINE
Assess whether you are doing all that you can to reach your goals without harming anyone along the way (including self).
Note: Discipline prevents punishment and pain!

COMPASSION
The ability to walk in the other person's shoes and treat them as you want to be treated.
Note: Compassion is the true definition of walking the talk!

PERSEVERANCE
Prudent, goal-directed behavior.
Note: Never give up on your dreams; see it through!

SPEAKING WITH A CONSCIOUS TONGUE
Thinking about what you say and its effects.
Note: Before you say something negative count to 1 million!

SELFLESSNESS
Not focused on action for reward.
Note: Do what is right all the time!

CONTRIBUTE
Giving freely to assist in the maintenance of prosperity in education, fitting the guidelines of your academic institution
Note: GIVE: Self explanatory!

*Author Unknown

PART I
This is My Life

Name: _____ **Date:** _____

School/Program: _____

I was born in _____.

Even at the age of _____ I was a _____child.

I liked to _____ and _____.

I also liked to _____.

When I became a teenager, I _____.

In school I _____.

Outside of school I _____.

When faced with adversity, I _____

_____.

My view of myself is that I _____

_____.

As I grow/grew older and moved toward graduation from middle/high school, I began to
have the feeling that _____, so I decided to _____.

I think the reason I did what I did was that _____

_____.

At age 18 I will: _____.

At age 24 I will: _____.

At age 30 I will: _____.

The person who I will become: _____

_____

_____

_____

_____.

PART II
Pre/Post Assessment

Name: _____   **Date:** _____

School/Program: _____

1. What are your strengths? _____
_____
_____
_____
_____
_____
_____
_____

2. What areas do you think you need to improve? _____
_____
_____
_____
_____
_____
_____
_____

3. What do you think your parents, teacher(s) would say about you? _____
_____
_____
_____
_____
_____
_____
_____

4. What are your career aspirations? What steps are you taking to get there? _____
_____
_____
_____
_____
_____
_____
_____

5. Do you have a mentor? If yes, identify your mentor. _____
_____
_____
_____

If no, please seek one immediately.

PART III
Personality Index

Name: _____ **Date:** _____

School/Program: _____

1. Do you prefer to be at home or out and about? _____

2. Do you prefer to be talking or listening? _____

3. Do you prefer to be listening or reading? _____

4. Which study method do you prefer; group, with a friend, or alone? _____

5. Which study method is most productive? _____

6. Would you rather write a position paper or give a report? _____

7. Would you rather produce an album or sing on the album? _____

8. When listening to music, which is most important to you, the lyrics or the beat? _____

9. Which way do you learn a skill best; observing examples, listening to instructions, or reading instructions? _____

10. What's your preferred method of communicating: face to face, email, text, phone, Twitter, facebook? _____

11. Do you read instructions first or try to figure out how to fix things first? _____

12. Are you a morning person or a night person? _____

PART IV
100% Attitude

Name: _____ Date: _____

School/Program: _____

Explain how a person with a positive attitude would respond to each writing prompt.

Van tends to exaggerate things by viewing a setback as a pattern of things to come in his career. Van took The ACT test for the first time with no practice. When he received a 23 on his ACT score report, he was not certain that he would be able to improve his score. Van said, "these test are biased and they tend to favor suburban rich kids." If Van had a more positive attitude, he would have handled this situation like this: _____
_____
_____
_____
_____

Manny is uncertain about his initiatives, assuming that his peers are critical of him. He started a community service program for feeding the senior citizens but did not get enough volunteers for a Saturday event. He made a comment in the community newspaper, "All my friends must think that my program is not good." If Manny had a more positive attitude, he would have handled this situation like this: _____
_____
_____
_____
_____
_____

Your attitude determines how far you go in life. Your attitude is a vital sign that you should check and monitor frequently.

A = Achievement
T = Time management
T = Trust
I = Impervious
T = Truth
U = Unequivocal
D = Dream
E = Excellence

Part V
Values

Name: _____ **Date:** _____

School/Program: _____

The thing I like best about myself is _____
_____
_____

The changes I would like to see in myself, in my environment, at my school, and at my job
are _____
_____
_____

In the next five years, I know I will be _____
_____
_____
_____

I need to meet and sit down and have dinner with _____
and why _____
_____
_____
_____

What I will accomplish in life is _____
_____
_____
_____

What I enjoy most about life is: _____
_____
_____
_____

Name the top four things you value most

1.

2.

3.

4.

Academic Achievement
and Personal Development
Action Plan (AAPD)

Never confuse movement with action.
Either do or do not. There is no try.
– author unknown

Name: _____ Date: _____

School/Program: _____

I. Goal(s): What I want to accomplish?

II. Actions: What steps do I need to take to make it happen?

1._____   5._____

2._____   6._____

3._____   7._____

4._____   8._____

III. Barriers to Success: What is in the way?

1._____   5._____

2._____   6._____

3._____   7._____

4._____   8._____

IV. Resource
What do I already have that can help me?   What do I need to accomplish my goal?

1._____   1._____

2._____   2._____

3._____   3._____

4._____   4._____

5._____   5._____

V. Support

Whom will I ask for support?

1._____
2._____
3._____
4._____

How can others help me?

1._____
2._____
3._____
4._____

VI. What can my parents, guardian(s), mentor(s), and school staff do to help me?

1._____
2._____
3._____
4._____

VII. Commitment: What will I actually do?

1._____
2._____
3._____
4._____

VIII. Timeline: When will I take action?

Action	Date
1._____	_____
2._____	_____
3._____	_____
4._____	_____
5._____	_____

Keys to Developing the AAPD Action Plan

Establishing and building the characteristics of a highly motivated and high achieving student is a monumental task. It is predicated upon the identifiable factors that contribute to the personal development plan implemented for successful outcomes for the individual student. It is important to note that this framework is a process that should be tailored to meet the needs of anyone who is seeking to achieve academically and improve personally. It is also important to note that these plans will vary based on the needs assessment of the individual and his/her goals and objectives.

I have established a **RAP Framework** for constructing and building the characteristics of highly motivated and high-achieving students. This process requires you to talk to yourself frequently about building a personal blueprint for success.

R   Reflect

- Come to terms with your current condition, then identify desired conditions for yourself. Construct a personal vision, mission, and success plan.

- Take inventory of your personal involvement in programs and work with your parents, peers, adults/mentors, and school staff to identify the pros and cons related to achieving your goals..

- Establish realistic expectations for yourself and support mechanisms needed from your parents, peers, adults/mentors, and school staff.

A   Assess your Needs

- Assess local, national, and international data on yourself and your peer group for a summation of trend analyses associated with student achievement. This data will yield external recommendations of the next steps to fix internal challenges. However, it is you who must decide for yourself.

- Collect and analyze that data to determine the gaps between where you are and where you need to be. The gaps will automatically identify your needs. Prioritize your needs based on your vision, mission, and success plan.

P   Plan

- Establish short and long-term goals.

- Identify measurable objectives for personal development.

- Identify multi-faceted strategies, activities, and actions parallel to expected outcomes to your personal development plan. Your strategies should:

  - directly relate to achieving your goals and objectives

  - identify persons responsible/accountable and resources needed for implementation

  - include the involvement and active participation of your parents, peers, adults/mentors, community members, and school staff

  - include a continuous accountability and evaluation process with benchmarks and timelines

  - include plans for personal development

Don't worry about talking to yourself.
Worry when you're not talking to yourself or listening.
– author unknown

Epilogue

Kevin Harris, Ed. D.
October 1, 1970 –
The Thursday Child

You are presented with an opportunity to become a transcendent pathfinder. You can go beyond ordinary limits when you are fully engaged in what you were destined to be involved in. You have come to a point where you have to make a decision that involves sacrificing your comfort for the good of others, even when there is no certainty of return. You engage readily in social and political resistance. You are able to go ahead with what you must be doing, gradually and individually every day, even if it means sitting on an accident waiting to happen. Yours is always a brave and courageous act with a religious foundation. The risks you take may not always make you a winner, but you achieve the ends of society even if you merely raise the level of discourse. You make all of us more confident in our ability to know what is right. You make people see their collective vocation to build and develop their community in an effort to restore people to their traditional greatness. You are a strong one—strong in will power and in political leadership.

Still less room is there for those who deride or slight what is done by those who actually bear the brunt of the day; nor yet for those others who always profess that they would like to take action, if only the conditions of life were not what they actually are. The man who does nothing cuts the same sordid figure in the pages of history, whether he be cynic, or fop, or voluptuary. There is little use for the being whose tepid soul knows nothing of the great and generous emotion, of the high pride, the stern belief, the lofty enthusiasm, of the men who quell the storm and ride the thunder. Well for these men if they succeed; well also, though not so well, if they fail, given only that they have nobly ventured, and have put forth all their heart and strength.

It is not the critic who counts; not the man who points out how the strong man stumbles, or where the doer of deeds could have done them better. The credit belongs to the man who is actually in the arena, whose face is marred by dust and sweat and blood; who strives valiantly; who errs, and comes short again and again, because there is no effort without error and shortcoming; but who does actually strive to do the deeds; who knows the great enthusiasms, the great devotions; who spends himself in a worthy cause; who at the best knows in the end the triumph of high achievement, and who at the worst, if he fails, at least fails while daring greatly, so that his place shall never be with those cold and timid souls who know neither victory nor defeat.

There is no more unhealthy being, no man less worthy of respect, than he who either really holds, or feigns to hold, an attitude of sneering disbelief toward all that is great and lofty, whether in achievement or in that noble effort which, even if it fails, comes second to achievement.

–Theodore "Teddy" Roosevelt (1913)

Uncle Mickey Harris
and a host of others helped me find my way...
What are you going to do?

REFERENCES

Anson, A. R., Cook, T. D., Habib, F., Grady, M., Haynes, N. M. & Comer, J. P. (1991). The Comer School Development Program: A theoretical analysis. *Journal of Urban Education, 26,* 56-82.

Anyon, J. (1995). Race, social class and educational reform in an inner city school. *Teachers College Record, 97,* 69-94.

Apple, M. W. (1995). *Ideology and curriculum.* Boston: Routledge & Kegan Paul.

Beauboeuf-Lafontant, T. (1999). A movement against and beyond boundaries: "politically relevant teaching" among African American teachers. *Teachers College Record, 100,* 702-723.

Bourdieu, P. (1977). Cultural reproduction and social reproduction. In Karabel & A. H. Halsey (Eds.), *Power and ideology in education* (pp. 487-511). New York: Oxford University Press.

Boykin, A. W. (in press-b). Talent Development, cultural deep structure and school reform: Implications for African Immersion initiatives. In D. Pollard & C. Ajirotutu (eds.), *Sankofa: Issues in African-centered education. Westport*: Greenwood.

Boykin, A. W. (1996, April). *A talent development framework for middle and high school reform.* Paper presented at the annual meeting of the American Education Research Association, New York.

Byrk, A., Sebring, P., Kerbow, D., Rollow, S., & Easton, J. (1998). *Charting Chicago school reform.* Boulder: Westview Press.

Calabrese, R. L. (1990). The public school: A source of alienation for minority parents *Journal of Negro Education, 59(2),* 148-154.

Catteral, J. S. (1996). Risk and resilience in student transitions to high school. *America Journal of Education, 106,* (February), 302-333.

Coleman, J. S. (1987). Families and schools. *Educational Researcher, 17,* 32-38.

Coleman, J. S. (1988). Social capital in the creation of human capital. *American Journal of Sociology, 94,* S95-S120.

Coleman, J. S., & Hoffer, T. (1987). *Public and private high schools: The impact of communities.* New York: Basic Books.

Comer, J. P. (1986). Parent participation in the schools. *Phi Delta Kappa,* February, 442-446.

Cook, T. D., Habib, F., Phillips, M., Setterson, R. A., Shagel, S. C., & Degirmencioglu, S. M. (1999). Comer's school development program in Prince Georges County, Maryland: A theory-based evaluation. *American Educational Research Journal, 36(3),* 599-607.

Darling-Hammond, L. (2000). teacher quality and student achievement: A review of state policy evidence. *Education Policy Analysis Archives, 8(1).* Retrieved from http://epaa.asu.edu/epaa/v81/

131

Dow, I. L., & Oakley, W. F. (1992). School effectiveness and leadership. *Alberta Journal of Educational Research, 38(1)*, 33-47.

Edmonds, R. (1979). Effective schools for the urban poor. *Educational Leadership, 37*, 15-27.

Epstein, J. L. (1994).Theory to practice: School and family partnerships lead to school improvement and success. In C. Fagnano & B. Werber, (Eds.), *School, family and community interaction: A view from the firing lines* (pp. 39-54). Boulder: Westview Press.

Giroux, H. A. (1983). *Theory & Resistance in Education.* London: Heinemann Educational Books.

Giroux, H. A. (1983). *Theories of reproduction and resistance in the new sociology of education:* A critical analysis. South Hadley: Bergin and Garvey.

Gratz, D. B. (2000). High standards for whom? *Phi Delta Kappan, 81*, 51-84.

Hale-Benson, J. (2001). *Learning while black: Creating educational excellence for African American children.* Baltimore: The Johns Hopkins University Press.

Irvine, J. J. (1991). *Black students and school failure: Policies, practices, and prescriptions.* New York: Praeger.

Jones, R. L. (1989). *Black adolescents.* Berkeley: Cobb & Henry.

Kunjufu, J. (1986). *Countering the Conspiracy to Destroy Little Black Boys, Vol. II.* Chicago: African American Images:

Lee, C. V. (1984). An investigation of psychosocial variables related to academic success for rural black adolescents. *Journal of Negro Education, 53*, 424-434.

Lomoty, K. (1990). *Going to school.* New York: State University of New York Press.

Losen, D., & Orfield, G. (2002). *Racial Inequality in Special Education.* The Civil Rights Project. Boston: Harvard University Press.

MacLeod, J. (1987). *Ain't No Making It: Aspirations & Attainment in a Low-Income Neighborhood.* Oxford: Westview Press, Inc.

Mauer, Marc (1995) *Young Black Americans and the Criminal Justice System: Five Years Later.* Washington, DC: The Sentencing Project.

McCombs, B. L., & Whisler, J. S., (1997). The Learner-centered classroom and school: Strategies for enhancing student motivation and achievement. V. Thomas (Ed.), Learner-Centered Alternatives to Social Promotion and Retention: A Talent Development Approach. *Journal of Negro Education, 69(4)*, 2000.

McLoyd, V. (1990). The impact of economic hardship on Black families and children: Psychological distress, parenting, and socio-emotional development. *Child Development, 61*, 311-346.

Noddings, N. (1984). *Caring: A feminine approach to ethics.* University of California Press.

Oakes, J. (1985). *Keeping track: How schools structure inequality.* New Haven: Yale University Press.

Pine, G. J., & Hilliard, A. G. (1990). Rx for racism: Imperatives for America's schools. *Phi Delta Kappa, 56,* 593-600.

Prom-Jackson, S., Johnson, S., & Wallace, M. (1987). Home Environment, Talented Minority Youth and School Achievement. *Journal of Negro Education, 56,* 111-121.

Roosevelt, T. (1913). *History as literature and other essays.* New York: Charles Scribner'sSons.

Rosenholtz, S. (1989). *Teacher's workplace: The social organization of schools.* New York: Longman.

Sarason, S. B. (1982). *The Culture of the School and the Problem of Change.* (2nd Ed.). Boston: Allyn & Bacon. (Originally published in 1971).

Senge, P. (1990). *The Fifth Discipline.* New York: Doubleday.

Sergiovanni, T. J. (1990). Adding value to leadership gets extraordinary results. *Educational Leadership, 47(8),* 23-27.

Sowell, Thomas. (1974) "Black Excellence: The Case of Dunbar High School." *Public Interest 35,* 1-21.

Smith, Rosa A. (2005). "Saving Black Boys: Unimaginable Outcomes for the Most Vulnerable Students Require Imaginable Leadership." *School Administrator,* v62 n1 p16.

Stanton-Salazar, R. (1997). "A social capital framework for understanding the socialization of racial minority children and youths." *Harvard Educational Review, 67, 1,* 1-40.

Steinberg, L. (1996). *Beyond the classroom.* New York: Simon & Schuster.

Thomas, V. G. (2000). Learner-Centered Alternatives to Social Promotion and Retention: A Talent Development Approach. *The Journal of Negro Education, 69(4),* 323-337.

Toldson, Ivory. (2010): "Understanding African American Adolescent Males Who Succeed." *The Newsmagazine: Howard University School of Education, 1,* 4-5.

Werner, E. E., and Smith, R. S. (1982). *Vulnerable but invincible: A longitudinal study of resilient children and youth.* New York: McGraw-Hill.

Wilson, Amos N. (1992). *Awakening the Natural Genius of Black Children (2nd Ed).* New York, NY: Afrikan World Infosystems.

Wynn, J., Richman, H., Ruinstein, R. A., Little, J., Britt, B., & Yoken, C. (1987). *Communities and adolescents: An exploration of reciprocal supports.* Unpublished report prepared for the William T. Grant Foundation Commission on Work, Family and Citizenship: You and America's Future.

Yukl, G. A., (1998). *Leadership in Organizations* (4th ed.). Upper Saddle River: Prentice Hall.

Speaking Engagements, Trainings, Book Discussions

Kevin Harris, Ed.D.
Harris Enterprise International, LLC
www.harriseillc.com
kharrisenterprises@gmail.com
Phone 404.647.4846
Phone 216.905.1867
Fax 404.627-5023

As an independent consultant, my pedigree includes providing personalized educational, training, and speaking services. I provide these services in one-on-one, seminar, and colloquium settings. My audiences include students, school leadership personnel, teachers, parents, corporations, colleges/universities, and community/faith-based organizations. I highly recommend job-embedded activities where real-time coaching and mentoring exist and lead to rich reflections and opportunities to learn and develop good practices.

My mission is to conduct interactive/collaborative needs assessments and utilize research to construct new thinking and apply effective practices to transform the overall efficiency for each client by exceeding standards while delivering quality services.

Offering student and staff training classes

Improving Students from Within
The internal (intrinsic) motivation that yields the
external (extrinsic) outcomes

Building Community in Self
Tools students need for a sustainable academic career
at his/her college/university of choice

Leadership in Empowered Students
Traits & Aspirations for Building Profiles in Excellence

Working on the Work
An Academic Achievement and Personal Development Action Plan
for Students who Choose to Succeed

Upcoming Publications

Existential Thoughts – Postmodern Actions:
Overstanding the Elements and Epistemology of the
Education System in the Urban Terrain

The College Student: The Life, Liberty and Pursuit of Debt-Freedom

Trial and Error: A Photo Story on the Anxiety and Joys of
Fathers Raising Black Boys